D1737432

Shaken Dreams

A Journey from Wife
to Caregiver

Holly Bird

SHAKEN DREAMS

A Journey from Wife to Caregiver
By Holly Bird

Copyright © 2018. All rights reserved.

No part of this publication may be reproduced, distributed, or
transmitted in any form or by any means, including photocopying,
recording, or other electronic or mechanical methods, without
the prior written permission of the publisher, except in the case
of brief quotations embodied in critical reviews and certain other
noncommercial uses permitted by copyright law.

Transcendent Publishing
PO Box 66202
St. Pete Beach, FL 33736
www.transcendentpublishing.com

Transcendent
Publishing

ISBN: 978-1-7932468-1-3

Printed in the United States of America.

DEDICATION

To my husband, Malcom Timothy "Tim" Bird: For the love and joy that you brought to me in my life, your children that loved me and I love as my own, and this journey we have all traveled together.

My daughter Dolly, my mother Ann, and my father Howard: I thank each of you for your love and support. You have given me the greatest gift I can imagine.

I love you all.

TABLE OF CONTENTS

INTRODUCTION

We all have struggles in our lives that take us on a journey of many ups and downs. At a time when my life was finally on a path of happiness and success, my journey took a detour of frustration and pain. I had seen and helped others go through difficult times, but I never expected to find myself on a path of so much uncertainty and confusion.

Having a chronic illness myself and finding out that the love of my life—who'd always been there to support me—would now need my help was life-changing, but it was also a common human experience. In our lives, we all go through times when we have to be there for someone else, even though we don't know how or even *if* we will be able to do it.

After four years of living through the many questions and the guilt of a journey that took my whole family down the proverbial rabbit hole, I felt that others could learn from this journey. I knew I could provide a much-needed guide for others dealing with chronic illness and caregiving, and—most of all—I could help others with the questions we forget to ask, the ones that can make a difference in how we handle and advocate for ourselves and loved ones during an illness.

CHAPTER 1

As I sat on my bed, I could feel the softness of the down comforter surrounding my body, cradling my 51-year-old body with a comforting hug that I needed. It was the first time in days that I'd had any feelings in my life. I had been in a daze, emotionally and physically, and now I could feel my eyes starting to burn. I tried to close them, to stop the pain, and immediately fell asleep. At that moment, my eyes stopped burning, but the dreams—some might call them nightmares—started.

Laughter and joy had always filled our home. We might have had a few disagreements, but never any arguments, and never in front of the children. We owned a small but successful wholesale distribution company. Tim had pleaded with me for two years to join him in his business venture, and finally, I did. His dream was to retire before his sixtieth birthday so we could travel and see the world. At that time, I didn't know it would be one of the best decisions of my life, even though some would say being together for twenty-four hours a day could be rough on a marriage. Not only did this make us great business partners, but my husband was my best friend. We were each other's whole world, and life was great!

When we first met, Tim had just had his forty-third birthday, and I was almost forty years old. I had one daughter, age sixteen, who was going through some major problems with self-image and confidence. Tim had four children of his own. The oldest was in her twenties, already out on her own and on her chosen career path. She was so wonderful to be around, and I felt a closeness to her from the first time

I met her. His son was seventeen. He was struggling with some life decisions that would affect him for a long time, and at that time, he still needed a lot of guidance and support. These two adult children came from his first marriage. Their mother lived out-of-state.

Tim's two youngest daughters were nine and four years old, and I fell in love with the joy and happiness they always seemed to carry with them. Sometimes, over the years, it has seemed to me that I fell in love with them before I did with Tim. The oldest of the two was a little caregiver with a huge heart and open to being loved. The youngest was so special—she wanted to be loved. She hugged me the first time we met and said, "You beaut-ful." Though she struggled with her speech, it made her extra cute. From the day I met them, I could feel the motherly side of me so filled with joy as our relationship grew and got stronger. The girls were with us most of the time since their mom was having some difficulties of her own.

Because of my own experiences with divorce and children, I had mentored many divorced couples, and Tim knew this from the beginning. My belief was never to talk badly about the children's other parent and to encourage the children to have a loving relationship with each parent. Just because you are getting a divorce, your children don't have to hear all the bad things you and your ex might be feeling at the time!

Our lives were full, and with so many in our family and our last name being Bird, I always called our home the "Bird Nest."

Every morning when I wake up, as I lie in bed, I can remember that day as if it were yesterday. Tim and I were asleep in bed, and something woke me from my sleep. I looked over and saw my husband was still fast asleep, so I knew—or at least I thought—it was too early. He was like a morning rooster. At 4:30 every morning, he would touch me and say, "You up?"

I am now, is what I would think, as I'd move slowly to get out of bed. It would be time to start the day at our wholesale company for the automotive paint and body industry. It seemed that getting up early was a prerequisite for this industry—or that's what Tim made me believe.

In my memory of that one morning, as I looked through hazy eyes toward the alarm clock, all of a sudden, it went off. I was surprised! The alarm had never gone off in the seven years since I had joined Tim in the business. I reached over and touched him, asking, "You up?"

He replied, "Are you trying to take my job?"

I smiled. Somehow, I knew it was going to be a good day. Tim was already making me smile, something I looked forward to every day.

Life was different for us. We'd both had multiple marriages, and I had been life-coaching families and couples to help them through different situations in their lives, everything from personal goals to nursing home admissions. I had seen so many situations, I just knew I was finally with the man I wanted to spend the rest of my life with. Even though I wasn't sure what that was going to look like, it felt right. I had never really felt this way before in my life. It felt good, and I was finally seeing that all my dreams of finding a life partner were coming true, something I had thought for years would never happen.

Over twenty years before we met, my life changed. I was diagnosed with MS—multiple sclerosis—which not only gave me problems, called flares, but also made some of my days very difficult, especially when it got hot outside. We lived in Arizona, so some years were worse than others. Tim was all in and even helped with the heavy stuff like laundry and groceries. He would say, "Your job is to make our business and life happy and successful." Helping others had always been my first love, and marketing and sales had always been what I was good at. Sometimes, it felt like Tim put me on a pedestal, even though I knew I shouldn't be there, but I truly enjoyed his appreciation.

On that morning, getting out of bed, I watched Tim slowly pull himself up and then out of bed. Then he lost his balance and said, "Whoa! I haven't even been drinking yet."

I laughed a little because Tim never really drank much. I didn't think too much about it as I had balance problems all the time. Tim never reminded me of my "problems" with my MS, so I was trying not to show too much concern, even though I was surprised.

As he walked through the doorway into the bathroom, he stopped and stood silently for a few seconds. All of a sudden, he walked through the doorway into the bathroom, looked back at me, and said, "That was weird. It was like someone stopped me, and I couldn't move for a minute."

I wasn't sure what he was trying to say, but this morning was so very different from every other morning over the last seven years. It was a little scary, but I didn't say anything, I just continued to watch him as we got dressed.

Driving to work that morning, he was unusually quiet. He would usually talk about the day, reminding me of all the people I had to call about sales and collections. Today, he said nothing. I could barely hear him breathing. This quiet was so different, almost frightening, but I didn't know why I was feeling this way. I just knew that something was wrong. I kept going through what had happened earlier in the morning.

It was making my mind spin.

I had to break the silence. "So, do you think one of our spirits was playing with you this morning?" Both of us had always believed that we had energy around us from people who had passed away. Sometimes, lights would go off and on by themselves, or we'd smell what Tim had told me was his mother's perfume in the house. I had never met her as she passed away at an early age from lymphoma, but I certainly smelled the perfume.

I looked over at him and noticed he wasn't smiling. Something was really bothering him. Then he quietly said, "I don't know what that was this morning, but it was strange, even for me." And then the van was quiet again.

The drive usually took only about thirty minutes, but that morning, it seemed to take forever. As we pulled up to the back-loading dock of our business, he grabbed my hand and said, "You know I love you, right?"

I was shocked, not at what he'd said, but how it was said.

Answering him, I tried not to show concern, only love. "I do. Your love has changed my life." I was really worried. His behavior had never frightened me before, but today, everything seemed different, somehow.

I squeezed his hand and said, "Now, let's get to work." Smiling, I added, "My wake-up service was late today." I saw a small answering smile on his face, but my heart was heavy. I could tell something was truly bothering my husband, who was always problem-free and believed that each day was, in his words, "Awesome!"

CHAPTER 2

A couple of weeks passed, but the mornings continued to be strained. I noticed his body and his voice were getting shakier. I started to push him, looking for answers. "You need to go have some blood work done." I tried not to say the "D" word—you'd think that hearing the word "doctor" would give someone hope that they might get some answers to what was going on, but Tim was the opposite. He was a pusher. He would even push me, saying things like, "Just get up and move." He'd tell me with love in his heart, "Our bodies aren't meant to lie still." However, he had trust issues with anything that had to do with going to a doctor.

Some days, I found it difficult to function, especially having a chronic illness. Tim, on the other hand, was the type of person who had even gone to work with a fever of 102, and I knew that when it came to his health, he didn't trust anyone. I had always believed this was because of his mother's early death, along with the information he had learned later about the cause of her lymphoma after she'd passed away. It was the way the doctors handled and answered questions about her death. They simply said nothing "Because no one asked", and this had really affected Tim and the way he felt about the medical profession as a whole.

With all the changes in Tim, I started searching on the internet about the symptoms I was seeing. In our industry, these could be caused environmentally from fumes and toxins that we are around every day. Reassuringly, most of the information I could find said that, caught in time, the problems could be fixed if the toxin could be identified.

The more I read, the more Parkinson's seemed to come up, but in almost everything I was reading, it only happened in older people, not in a forty-seven-year-old. I also knew that some of these symptoms had been around for a couple of years, just never at the same time. I shared what I'd found with Tim and told him that we really needed to have this looked at, especially if it might be environmental. A few months prior, his older brother, only a couple years older than Tim, had been diagnosed with Parkinson's.

I was hoping that we might simply need to make some adjustments in our business for the sake of his health, but I struggle with believing in coincidences, and I was worried. My main goal was getting an appointment with his primary care doctor. When I told Tim this, he tried to be funny and said, "I have one of those?" I knew this was going to be a struggle, but I set the appointment and made sure our schedule was cleared. He was going—even if I had to drag him.

Since Tim had never been to his primary care doctor before, he was nervous. The whole time we were driving there, he was trying to get out of going. Of course, I wasn't listening, so he tried one last thing when we got to the office. As we walked to the door, he saw the name on the window and said, "She's a woman?!"

I smiled and agreed, "Usually someone named Susan is a woman."

I could see a bit of panic in his eyes, and I tried to reassure him that everything would be okay, that this was just a first meeting to see how we liked her and whether she could get us a referral to a specialist.

I could tell by the look in his eyes that he wasn't convinced.

After we checked in and filled out all the paperwork, the medical assistant took us back to the exam room. She was trying to stay focused, but after Tim had teased her about his weight and what a strong man he was, she was a bit distracted. She opened up a drawer, grabbed a dark purple gown, and said in a no-nonsense voice, "Everything off except underwear."

Tim looked at me as she closed the door and said, "No female doctor is playing with my balls!"

I knew this was going to be a long afternoon, and I was really trying not to laugh. I kept thinking in the back of mind, *if he keeps this up, no one will want to help us*, and, *Maybe I should have found a male doctor*—because sometimes Tim's sense of humor wasn't so funny to others, especially women.

The doctor came into the room. She was a short, nice-looking, middle-aged Asian woman, and she had a deep voice that I wasn't expecting. "Good afternoon, Mr. Bird. How are you today?"

I looked over at Tim and saw the gleam in his eye. I knew what he was going to tell her. All of a sudden, he pointed at me and said, "Because she thinks I need someone to take some blood and play with my balls." I couldn't believe it—well, I guess I could. Tim was always free and open-mouthed with his thoughts.

The doctor turned and looked at me, burst out laughing, and said, "It's nice to meet you!" From that moment, I knew we had the right doctor!

We sat with that doctor for over two hours in an appointment that had been scheduled for forty-five minutes. She took the time to get to know both of us as a couple, and that was when Tim found out she would also be the primary doctor for me and for the girls. It made him feel better to know she would treat us as a family, and I wasn't "picking" on him—his words when he didn't want to do something.

Even though both of us had started to build a newly found confidence in our doctor, we would have to wait for the blood work to come back to see the levels of toxicity. She didn't really believe that

Tim had Parkinson's because the average age of onset is 60, and only 1 in 100 people are affected. She did point out that a movie star had been diagnosed as having early onset but mentioned that this was rare. She explained that Parkinson's disease was caused by low dopamine levels. Not even the experts knew why this happened, but it usually occurred only in older people.

We left the office still feeling unsure of what was causing Tim's symptoms. He was frustrated, feeling that the doctor might be trying to hide something from us. These insecure feelings couldn't be fixed. All I could do was try to reassure him that I felt she was going to be honest with us. He wasn't so sure.

We were surprised when all the blood work came back normal. Over the prior weeks, it had seemed that his tremor was getting more prominent, especially when he was resting. I was exhausted from watching him. He would try to sit on his hands or put them in his pockets so no one could see the tremors, even though it made the problem more obvious.

This was in 2008, and no medical testing involving a blood draw or machine was available, so the doctor referred Tim to see a neurologist. Anticipation was building, and Tim was feeling upset and agitated. Even though he wanted to quit talking about it, he finally admitted that he had been feeling shaky inside for "a while" and that lately, he was always feeling sore and stiff from work.

It was over a six-week wait to get in to see the neurologist. Tim was wanting to be done—he felt that focusing on his health was making him nervous, and he was struggling both at work and at home. The man who had all the patience in the world and loved being around family and friends had quit smiling. His sense of humor was lost in a whirlwind of frustrations, and the slightest thing would make him angry.

I just tried not to talk about his health.

We finally got in to see the neurologist. The doctor was a small man. Even his hands were like a child's. He was abrupt, and almost rude, as he did a couple of pokes with his tools and had Tim walk down the narrow hallway. Less than five minutes into the appointment, he asked Tim, "Why are you here? What is your problem?" These were his first questions.

Tim looked over at me and said, "Ask her. I am fine, just a little shaky on some days." He added, "I also seem to get frustrated more easily than I used to."

Well, I didn't know if I was going to cry, yell, or just walk out of the room. I took a deep breath and gathered my composure so I could start explaining what was going on. I talked about my concerns, worries, and our business, including all the chemicals that Tim was around every day and the fact that Tim was driving a commercial box truck with hazardous items. I wanted to make sure he was safe and other people wouldn't get hurt. I wanted to know if these symptoms could affect his driving, and of course, what was causing them. I felt as if I explained the situation well, as well as my true concerns for Tim and all the changes I could see that were going on.

The doctor stood up and held out his hand to shake Tim's hand. He said, "Your bloodwork was fine. There was nothing toxic. You appear to be a healthy man; you are fine." He paused for a moment and continued, "Maybe if you got rid of *her*, all your symptoms would go away."

I was devastated, shocked, and truly hurt. I hadn't even had a chance to tell the doctor about Tim's brother. When I looked up, I saw Tim smiling. It wasn't his usual smile, but it was the first one I'd seen in a month. He said to me, "I told you nothing was wrong!"

A few weeks went by, and to my dismay, Tim told everyone that story. I continued to watch for symptoms. I could see them increasing, and we still had no answers—well, at least, I didn't. Tim was happy to know that a neurologist had merely felt he was suffering from a little depression, that he didn't need medication—maybe just a divorce.

On one of those nights when Tim's symptoms were bad, I went to bed knowing that the stress was causing my health to take a turn for the worse, so I meditated. I tried to focus on myself. I knew that I had to let things go until Tim was ready to acknowledge that there was a problem and that he needed help. As I cried myself to sleep, I kept wondering what had happened to the laughter? What had happened to our dreams that now seemed to be turning into a nightmare?

Our lives continued: taking the kids to school on our way to work, picking them up on our way home, softball practice, band concerts, birthday parties. It seemed that every time we saw someone we hadn't seen in a while, they would pull me aside and say that Tim wasn't looking very well—they would question whether he was okay. My worries continued to silently grow as the symptoms reminded me every day that something wasn't right. Meanwhile, Tim kept trying to hide his tremors, which sometimes made things worse.

CHAPTER 3

O ver the next several weeks, I suffered some setbacks with my health, and this seemed to make Tim nervous. I wasn't recovering as quickly as I had before, and he wanted to know why. He pushed me about it for several days, and I finally broke down. Tears streaming down my face, I told him I was worried about him.

I reminded him that I had learned to cope with my chronic illness, but I had also gotten the help I needed so I could live my life as normally as possible. I told him I had seen so many changes in him and that I had been struggling to let it go. We had a family that needed us both, and everyone was concerned: It wasn't just me, but customers and friends—and most important, our children were now concerned.

Tim hadn't been sleeping well for months, and of course, when he woke up, I did too. I had thought that maybe this why he was struggling with concentrating, and his memory wasn't as sharp as it used to be. We would joke about this; he'd say, "I have CRS, I can't remember shit," or he would tease, "Were we supposed to have sex tonight? I can't remember." We had gotten a little of our playful side back, and I didn't want to rock the boat.

I was still waiting for him to tell me he needed help. I was hoping it would be sooner than later as the symptoms were worse than they had ever been.

After concerned telephone calls from our customers, and watching Tim, I finally started riding with him in the truck to make the deliveries. He would tell the customers that I was out "collecting," so they'd better pay their bills, but he knew in his heart I was worried. He also knew that the customers had been telling me about the problems he was having when making the deliveries. As a part of our service to the customer, we had par levels for inventory—we controlled that with a computer program, and mistakes were being made. His health was affecting not only our business but our customers' businesses as well. Our relationship with our customers over the years had become close and personal, and it was more out of concern for Tim that they started questioning me about what was really going on, or whether something was wrong.

We spent the new few weeks together 24/7, and he finally said, "I can't handle this anymore. What do I need to do to help you feel better and quit worrying? The neurologist told you I was fine."

I looked at him and said, "Go get a prostate exam."

He was stunned. "What you mean, a prostate exam?"

I said, "It's been six months, and you told the doctor you would come in for a complete physical exam."

Finally, after weeks of biting my tongue—and I'm sure I was rolling my eyes—words I had been waiting six months to hear finally came out of his mouth. "Set the appointment."

I think that was the first time in six months I felt a little relief. I could now try to set a plan in motion—this problem needed a resolution, and I was determined to find one.

The next day, I called the doctor's office to set an appointment, and I asked if I could leave the doctor a message on her voicemail. The assistant put me through to the doctor's line. I explained that we were coming in and I knew that she had received the report from the neurologist, but things had gotten worse. If she could just take a closer look, maybe she could bring up a second opinion to Tim. I wasn't sure what she would do, but I had to try. I was emotionally weakened, and this wasn't a good place for me to be. I only hoped that this time, someone would see what I was seeing.

Three days later, we were in the doctor's office waiting room, and Tim looked at me and said with a smirk on his face, "I took a shower."

I answered, "That's good."

He raised an eyebrow and said, "Are you gonna come back and watch?"

I'm not sure what my face looked like, but the laugh that came from deep inside him made the room rock. I started laughing, too, noticing that other patients were watching and listening, some not so happy—but he was happy.

As I watched him, I noticed that even though he was happy, there was no smile on his face. This was new. His smile was always so big when he laughed, and his hazel eyes always shone. I had thought he hadn't been smiling lately because he was sad, but now I could see he was losing his facial expressions. It looked as though he was wearing a mask.

I asked, "Why aren't you smiling?"

He said, "I am!" He didn't even know that this was happening— another symptom, suddenly appearing.

I kept thinking, *I hope the doctor can see this.*

As we went back to the exam room, he playfully joked with the nurses, and I could feel someone watching us. I glanced over my shoulder. The doctor was watching from her office. I knew she had heard my message because she gestured to me to ignore her. I could see she was watching closely as we walked into the exam room.

Tim hadn't noticed the doctor; he was too busy teasing the aide. Meanwhile, I was wondering what she was looking for as she watched us—but relieved she was watching.

As he undressed, Tim struggled to get his belt off. His hands were shaking, but of course, I thought that the jokes were only starting. I told him, "You're just nervous about a female doctor examining you."

As I looked up at him, he said, "Can you help me? My hands aren't working today."

This was the first time he'd asked for help. I quickly jumped up from my chair and was trying to help him when the doctor walked in.

Tim's chart was in her hands, and she looked up from behind her reading glasses. Before she could say anything, Tim said with a little chuckle, "She wants to watch and help."

The doctor asked me to sit down. I hadn't had a chance to help Tim with his belt, and he was still trying to unfasten it, and I could see the doctor watching with concern in her eyes.

My heart racing, I knew the doctor had seen something by the way she was handling herself.

The appointment wasn't what either of us had anticipated. It was worse.

After the prostate exam and the numerous bad-taste jokes that Tim had to tell during this exam, she asked Tim to get dressed and said she would be back in a couple of minutes.

It was more like twenty minutes. Tim was getting impatient, and then we heard a light knock as the doctor said from behind the door, "Are you dressed yet?"

Tim answered, "For about a week now." I could tell he was ready to get out of the office and go anywhere that wasn't where we were!

But as the doctor came into the room, by the look on her face, I wasn't sure where we were headed. She had a referral in her hand, and as she handed it to me, she looked at Tim and said, "Mr. Bird, I am not a neurologist, but I have worked with many patients." She paused and added, "Sir, you have Parkinson's. I have talked to a neurologist, who is waiting to see you this afternoon."

Tim looked at her with his wide eyes and, trying to make light of the situation, said, "I guess I am too late for that divorce." Here I was, sitting in shock that my worst nightmare had come true, and Tim was still trying to go back to what the original neurologist had told us. But as I looked at him, I could see in his eyes that reality was starting to set in, and at that that point, I was wondering if he had suspected this all along.

As we got in the van to drive to the new neurologist, Tim said, "I will give you fifty bucks if you take me home."

I didn't answer. I just kept driving.

The air in our van felt like a vacuum pack. It was hard to breathe, and it felt like waves were crashing over us. I grabbed Tim's hand and said, "Hey, you know I love you!"

He squeezed my hand back and said, "Yes, babe. I've just been trying to keep all this from you—I've known something was wrong."

At that point, I felt relieved but so angry that he'd been trying to hide this. Now all I could do was hope we could get some help, find out what was going on with his symptoms, and maybe get some medications to control them.

The new neurologist's office was nicely appointed, and Tim mumbled under his breath, "He got me in so fast, he must need a new chair for his office."

I understood what he was talking about. The crystal chandelier and French Provincial furniture didn't seem like the best choice for a doctor's office, it was way over the top. This apparently made Tim feel uneasy, not something I was hoping for. I wanted him to feel relaxed so he would feel comfortable about opening up to the doctor.

The medical assistant escorted us in as soon as we walked up to the check-in window and took us right to the doctor's personal office instead of the usual exam room. Within minutes, the doctor, a younger man in his early forties with a bright and genuine smile, walked in and greeted us as if we were family. At that point, I knew he wasn't the one who'd decorated his waiting room. "Hello, I am Dr. John. It's wonderful to meet you!"

Of course, Tim was still thinking about the chandeliers, and he said, sounding a little irritated, "I'm sure!"

I quickly touched his arm. He knew that was my sign—it meant "Be nice!"

The doctor looked at both of us and then focused on Tim. He said, "I've been reading and talking to your primary care doctor. I also looked at the notes from your first neurologist visit. I want to take a look at you and have you tell me what you think is going on."

Tim pointed to me and said, "She can tell you."

Dr. John shook his head and said, "I prefer that you tell me. It's important that I understand what you're thinking."

I sat quietly and tried not to make any movement or sounds as I had never heard Tim tell any doctor what he thought was going on. I wasn't sure if he was about to do a comedy act, or if this time he might really talk about what was happening. I definitely didn't want this doctor to think I was overreacting and Tim would be better off divorced!

I could see Tim was struggling. We sat there, the doctor and I quietly waiting for him to speak, for what felt like an hour, but it was only a minute or two before he spoke. He finally started to talk about his feelings, his fears, and his family history. One thing he told us about was a dynamite manufacturing plant that had been in his hometown in Utah. They had "accidently" leaked toxic chemicals into the water source and parts of the soil. Many people had fallen ill, his brother had been diagnosed as having Parkinson's, and his father had also showed symptoms but was never diagnosed. He continued his story, telling the doctor that his mother had passed away from lymphoma. They had lived in the canyon that had been directly contaminated, and he'd had fears for many years that he was suffering from this, but he'd never wanted to admit it. He told the doctor that he'd always struggled with different symptoms and wondered about it, but he had known there was nothing he could do. Worse, the illnesses others had suffered had all ended badly.

I was shocked. Watching the doctor listen, I could tell he already knew what was going on. I just wished he would tell *us*. He then asked Tim if he would mind walking back to an exam room.

As we walked through the doorway, Tim stopped. I thought he was going to say something, but he just stood there, just like that first morning when I started to notice his struggles, and many times since.

The doctor, behind us, asked in concern, "Tim, are you okay?"

There was no answer. I waited a few seconds to see what the doctor would say. We all stood in silence.

Finally, I touched Tim's arm. I had done that before when this had happened, and he would be able to continue walking. I wasn't sure why this worked, but it did. Tim would always say I had the "magic touch." Later, we would find out that "freezing" was a symptom of Parkinson's.

The doctor stayed quiet, and I just knew he was watching in the same way our primary care doctor had watched earlier. Even so, his breathing got a little deeper and louder as the exam went on, and I could tell he was struggling with just watching. This was probably one of the first times that I was quiet and not trying to be Tim's advocate.

I was worried enough just being his wife.

After an extensive exam, Tim looked at the doctor and said, "Do you think a divorce would help?" Even though he was exhausted, I could tell he was still trying to show his sense of humor.

The doctor tried to smile through his concern and asked Tim if this was something he was thinking about.

Tim answered, "I have done it twice before, and everything got better, but when I met Holly . . . She has been my answer to my prayers, so unless you think it's necessary, I'd like to keep her."

My heart jumped in my chest with joy. Even though it was an emotional appointment, it was so nice to know that Tim loved and cared about me so much. It felt wonderful to hear it, especially at this time. The teasing from the first neurologist appointment hadn't stopped, and this had made me feel uneasy for a while.

The doctor smiled and nodded. He seemed to be catching on to the type of relationship we had. His eyes softened as he started to speak. "Tim, I know you have been struggling for a while now, and you're not even fifty yet, but with your exam and all the things we've done today, I have to agree with your primary care doctor. You do have Parkinson's and with Lewy bodies."

Tim looked at him and said quickly, "Well, tell Lewy he can have his body back, I don't want it."

I gently grabbed his hand and asked the doctor what that meant. I wasn't even sure what he was talking about. Tim, of course, was trying to make light of the situation. He kept interrupting, which seemed to be the way he was coping—or not wanting to hear what was being said.

The doctor continued. He told us that Tim's smile disappearing was called masked facies, also known as hypomimia, and Lewy body was a form of dementia. There was no testing for this form of dementia, but it happened with some neurological diseases. Doctors diagnose this condition by considering symptoms and asking questions like the ones this doctor had asked Tim. He further explained that it was a type of progressive dementia that leads to a decline in thinking, reasoning, and independent function because of abnormal microscopic deposits that damage brain cells over time.

I still wasn't sure what the doctor was trying to tell us. Actually, I was numb.

As the doctor wrote out some prescriptions, he tried to explain everything, but neither of us heard anything he was saying. Hearing the word *dementia,* our minds seemed to float away. I had worked with many families to find the right nursing home for their loved ones when the caretaking got too hard. Dementia can be very difficult to deal with. Tim and I had talked many times about some of the families, and many times, we'd promised each other that we would never send the other to a nursing home. The doctor could tell by the looks on our faces that we were lost in thought and we would need some time to process everything.

He handed us the prescriptions and a stack of pamphlets. When he'd finished writing, he looked up and said, "Be careful looking on the internet. You have what is called early-onset Parkinson's. I feel you have probably had this since your early forties because of the advancement of your disease." He looked from one of us to the other and added, "Most of the internet is just basic knowledge and could be confusing. I would like to see you next week after you have had time to start your medication and have had a chance to process everything we've talked about."

He stood up, shook our hands, and walked us to the front. I really don't remember making the follow-up appointment, driving home, or even talking to each other.

CHAPTER 4

The next few days were a blur. Thank goodness the appointment had been on Friday, and we had the weekend to try and process everything we had heard.

Tim didn't want to say anything to the children. I struggled with this, but I wanted to give him a chance to sort out everything he was feeling. I also wanted to give us a chance to talk about how we would want to tell them.

Tim seemed confused and asked me to start looking things up on the internet. He was afraid that the doctor was trying to hide something from him, like the doctors had done with his mother.

I agreed. Even though I knew what the doctor had said, I thought I could try to see if there was anything that might help us, especially advice on how to talk to your children about Parkinson's.

All day Saturday, we talked, and we looked at everything we could find about Parkinson's on the internet. The doctor had been right. Most of the articles were about elderly patients. I had known this from looking up Tim's symptoms before we ever went to a doctor. One well-known Hollywood star had started a foundation in October 2000. He had been diagnosed with early-onset Parkinson's nine years earlier. He seemed to be doing well on his medications, and this gave us some hope that maybe some of our dreams—even though they had been shaken—could still come true.

We called all of the children late Saturday afternoon and asked them to come to Sunday dinner. Luckily, they were all available, which sometimes was difficult as three of the five were very busy in their own lives. They knew we had been to the doctor, though, and by all the text messages we had received since Friday, we knew they had been waiting to hear what was going on with Dad.

As I set the table, the two youngest were excited to have everyone coming for dinner. The youngest one looked at her dad and said, "I am so happy to see everyone. We have the best family in the whole world." I remember that as if it was just a few minutes ago. I was so worried about how this one night was going to affect the family for the rest of our lives. I had seen the struggles with my brother-in-law and his family and all the emotional pain they had experienced. I also knew that our children had seen what their cousins had been going through, the emotional roller coaster they had been on for the past two years.

Everyone showed up a little early. Tim and I sat at each end of the table, and I waited. I knew that Tim had wanted to tell them, but he finally looked up from his plate and said, "Momma has something she has to tell you!"

I got a lump in my throat and tried to fight back the tears. I hadn't been expecting him to turn the conversation over to me. I slowly started to explain what was going on, and that we didn't have a lot of answers. I also told them we were happy that the medication they had started Tim on, just a couple days earlier, seemed to be helping the tremors, and the last two nights, he had slept better than he had in a long time, and that we were hopeful.

I looked around the table. The second youngest had tears streaming down her face, and the oldest had dropped her fork and put her napkin over her eyes. Our son was the first to speak. "So, I guess I am going to get this since all the men in the family have it." It was more of a statement than a question.

I was caught off guard. I didn't know how to answer. I just knew that I had to assure him that within a few weeks, we would know more. I also said that one way or another, we would find a way to see if this was hereditary. I just didn't know how or when we would really know. I could tell he wasn't happy with the answer as he looked at his dad in frustration and disbelief.

The evening was filled with questions, and I tried to stay focused. I knew I had to try to let Tim answer some of the questions, but it became so overwhelming. I'm not sure what was asked, but when Tim spoke up and said, "Just think, I will be really good at shaking aerosol cans, so we will make more money for the business," I looked across the table and saw that he was trying to let the kids know he was still the same dad, funny and wanting to be there for them.

Silence fell over the table. At last, my daughter, the second oldest girl, and also in the medical field, spoke up and said, "Dad, we love you, and we'll all do just fine. There are so many medical advances! If the medication seems to be working already, that's great!" I'm not sure she believed it, but she tried, and it helped calm the other children, especially the two younger ones.

When the older children were leaving, Tim wanted each of them to know that he loved them and would always be there for them, that hopefully, everyone could adjust to the "New Dad." Each one of them hugged us, and as they did, I could feel each of them trembling. I heard them sniffling and knew they were scared—and so was I. We were all headed down a road that we didn't know where it would take us.

Monday, as I was driving us to the office, I kept hearing the words "early-onset" and "dementia" over and over in my head. I had heard about early-onset because Tim's brother had been diagnosed with the same thing, but I wasn't sure about the dementia. I had worked in a nursing home environment with patients who had Alzheimer's and dementia, as well as their families, and I wasn't seeing that as "our" situation.

As the morning continued, the doctor's office called to remind us of Tim's appointment. It was for Wednesday, and I was glad they'd called because I couldn't remember when we were supposed to go back. When we had left the doctor's office, I hadn't been hearing anything; we still had a business to run, and the only thing I was thinking about was Tim and what he was feeling. When I told him, they'd called to confirm his appointment, he glanced over at me and said, "Good thing they called. Since I have this Lewy guy taking over my brain, you are going to need help."

At that point, I knew I needed to start keeping track of the many appointments the doctor had talked about, and to help remind me. I knew I couldn't afford to miss anything. If I did, it could affect the business, and without our business, we wouldn't have the financial resources that we would need to keep a roof over our heads, take care of our children, and pay all the medical expenses. I would need to become Tim's advocate for his health care as he didn't seem to care at all. I wasn't sure if that was the denial or the dementia. As it was, my days were even more confusing, with even more questions.

By his remarks, I could tell that Tim didn't want to believe what the doctors were saying. I would need to make sure Tim and our family were taken care of. The more I was learning, the more I knew that things would have to change. As I thought about it, I had already been taking more responsibilities with the business before the diagnosis. Tim had seemed to stop caring as much, focusing more on socializing and being known in the industry. Tim was well-liked and looked up to, so I knew that this could get even more difficult, especially with Tim's refusal to accept what we were being told.

As we walked into the office, Tim headed back to the warehouse as he had done every day we'd been working together. He was simply going back to his normal routine, but for me—I could feel panic setting in. I didn't know how to handle the situation. Mondays were usually my day in the office to take care of the paperwork and schedule deliveries for us and our customers. Tim would go out on his own and spend the day delivering and helping our customers in the field. Because we were successful as a "mom-and-pop" business, the only people we had to fall back on were our children, who had their own careers. Even though the two youngest loved helping, were good with their dad, and had learned about the business, they were in middle school and high school.

I asked Tim if he would mind me coming with him that day, and I would handle my work from his computer in the truck. That would give us time to spend together. I could tell by the look in his eyes that he was uneasy. He always pulled at the brim of his cap and looked down when he felt he was being betrayed or someone was lying to him.

He answered with, "You do have collections to do, and I could use the help."

I could see humor in his eyes, but he never looked up from under his cap. I answered him with, "Thanks, they always love collections on Monday, and it makes me laugh to watch them squirm."

Tim finally looked up with a very small smile and said, "I love you."

The day went well. I watched Tim drive and how he handled the customers. He seemed to be doing well, and I was so happy that the medicine he was taking seemed to be helping his tremors and his "freezing" while he was working. Even some of the customers mentioned how great he looked and that "Tim was back." He did share with some of them what had happened over the weekend, and that the doctors had diagnosed him with Parkinson's, but the meds were helping, and they "couldn't get rid of him that easy." But not one time did he ever bring up the Lewy body dementia, and at that point, we hadn't really talked about it. Another factor was that I didn't want our customers to have any fears that Tim's illness could put their own businesses at risk. They were depending on us to keep their inventories on par to run their businesses.

I would spend the next several months struggling with my own health while knowing that, at any time, the dementia we kept hearing about could and *would* surface. Making sure the children were at ease with their dad became my priority. The children were accepting and loving to their dad, and we attended every event from band concerts to softball games and parent-teacher conferences. Our calendar was full, and we also tried to be there for our first grandson, babysitting and just trying to enjoy being grandparents.

In 2010, everything looked good. We had put in a swimming pool a couple years earlier, and we had outstanding credit. This was so important to me because I knew if we ever needed it, whether for business or health, we would have access to all the money we needed.

CHAPTER 5

We started into our second year of the diagnosis. The doctor visits had gone from monthly to as-needed. We were finally seeing things as our "new" life with Parkinson's. The kids became our first priority. Even the business seemed to be running smoothly. I had started riding daily with Tim. When the girls were out of school, they would ride with their dad so I could do inventory and the office tasks that needed to be done. We were in the office at seven and out by three at the latest. We were making more money than we ever had, and life seemed to be back to normal.

Tim had become a little quieter, but he seemed to have an interest in everything we were doing. One afternoon, I was surprised—or should I say shocked—when the doorbell rang, and it was an appraiser from the bank. Tim had contacted the bank to refinance the house. He had never mentioned this to me, and I didn't know why he would want to do such a thing. Of course, the bank would do anything "we" asked; we had never been late and had paid extra every month since we'd bought the home seven years earlier.

We had just gotten home from work. Tim jumped up from his recliner. Usually, he took a nap when we got home, but now, he said, "I will take care of this."

I was in a panic. Tim had never handled any of the bills or anything financial since we had been together. I tried not to show the fear, that in the back of my mind, I was wondering if he had done something. I asked the appraiser, "What are you looking for?"

He answered, "Mr. Bird requested a refinance for a lower interest rate."

I looked at Tim, and he was so proud that he'd surprised me. "I am going to help us lower our monthly payments!"

I said okay and shrugged my shoulders, thinking to myself, *why not, if it saves us money.* It was the bank that held our mortgage. It shouldn't be a problem. Our credit was excellent, and the lower interest rates would save us $300.00 a month. That could help pay for medications since so many weren't covered by insurance.

The appraiser finished his work, and before he left, he complimented our home and its beauty. He mentioned that we would be hearing from the bank about a decision within seven business days.

Tim smiled. Rubbing his hands together, he said, "We're in the money."

I smiled. I was so proud that he'd thought about finding a way to help us. I just wish I had known before he processed the paperwork—because the appraiser was wrong. Only three days later, we received a certified letter in the mail from our bank, stating that with the swimming pool loan and the recent housing decline, our house wasn't valued at what we owed. We needed to come up with eighty-five thousand dollars in thirty days—or they would foreclose.

I couldn't believe it. We had never been late. The bank knew we only had sixty thousand in savings, which we were trying to save just in case. They had the advantage over us: our credit cards and all of our banking went through them.

We had to find a way to get more money together, and fast. We were devastated. Worse, Tim started showing more signs of the dementia than I had seen to this point. He was angry at me for calling the bank for a refinance. "Why did you call them?' he asked.

I knew somehow that this might push him over the edge. I would not correct him, I stayed quiet, just hugged him, and said, "We've got this."

Even so, Tim knew, just as I did, that several of our friends had lost their homes in this terrible downturn of events. The banks were panicking and foreclosing on thousands of people across the country. Now we knew how they were doing it, and we were stuck right in the middle of their trap.

As the old saying goes, don't put all your eggs in one basket. We had done just that. Now we had to make a decision: try to come up with the money, or walk away, something I didn't want to do. This was our family home, the place we called our "Bird Nest," the one place where everyone felt comfortable and loved. The decision had to be made. In the end, there was no choice; we had to walk away. I spent days explaining to Tim and trying to convince myself. I knew that we couldn't risk putting every penny we had into a home when it might take years to recover the financial loss we would incur. In my heart, I understood we would need the money if Tim continued to get worse. We might even have to sell the business.

We were fortunate that my mom and uncle owned a beautiful home on a lake, across the street from my mom. Tim fell in love with the house and wanted to rent it. He was upbeat, happy at the thought he could fish every night from his own dock.

So, we walked away from our home. In less than a month from the day the appraiser had come in, we cleaned and made sure it was in excellent shape. So many others who lost their homes this way destroyed their houses, stole the appliances—some even burned them down. But I was proud of this home we were losing. I hoped that someone would love it the same way we did.

Our new home was wonderful. The girls were happy; all their friends lived close, and everyone loved to come to the new "Birds

Nest." We learned a few months later that our old home was sold at auction for fifty-six thousand dollars, two hundred thousand less than what we would have owed if we'd been able to come up with the money. The bank lost out on that one. A couple years later, we received a thousand dollars as a settlement that the government made the banks issue for their tactics and business practices. This was another slap in the face, and it made Tim so mad, he ripped the check up and said he never wanted to talk about it again.

CHAPTER 6

A few weeks after moving into the new house, I had seen some major changes in Tim. He was losing his temper, and the "freezing and shuffling" part of his Parkinson's wasn't as controlled as it had been. I had suffered a couple of flares and was put on an IV at home to help settle my symptoms. Tim kept blaming himself, but I reassured him that in less than three days, I would be feeling great—and I was. Steroids always helped me feel better, and that helped keep him calm. I had learned to hide my problems, or at least, I thought I had.

It was within a couple of weeks after my flare that I was sitting at the office. I hadn't heard from Tim most of the day. I thought he was just giving me a break, allowing me to work without being bothered, I was so far behind. Then the phone rang.

It was the bank that we used for business. I went to that bank every day and knew all the employees. The voice on the other line sounded familiar but nervous. "Holly, this is Deb at the bank."

I tried to acknowledge her with a simple hi, but she just kept talking. "Tim is at the bank," she said. "He's sitting in the drive-through, and he is frustrated." It sounded like she swallowed hard before continuing, "He's screaming at us to give him his money back, and we don't know what to do?"

My first thought was to say, *Well, give him his money,* but she continued, "He didn't give us a deposit so we don't know what he's talking about!"

I was having problems connecting my mouth to what my brain was thinking, when she raised her voice, saying, "Holly, should I call the police?"

I quickly answered, "No, just tell him you'll get some help and walk away. I'll be there in less than two minutes!"

The bank was across the street from our office. I ran out the door, not knowing what I was going to do. I jumped into the van, and as I pulled around the back of the bank, I could see that Tim had pulled into the drive-through in our big delivery truck from work. I could see his reflection in the side view mirror of the truck, the deep red flush on his face showed he was mad. Seeing him pulling at the brim of his cap, I knew he was struggling, and I had to do something quickly.

I jumped out of the van and walked over, saying in my most cheerful voice, "Hey, Babe, whatcha doing here?'"

He said, "I can't find the deposit."

Something was wrong. At no time in the last eight years had he taken one of our deposits in the big truck. This was a task we did together on our way home after work. His brain was telling him that he was supposed to be doing something he hadn't done in a long time.

My mind was spinning, and my heart was beating so hard that I felt my pulse pounding in my fingertips.

The day I had worried about for over two years was here—no warning, no reason. As I stood next to the truck, Tim looked at me and said, "What are you doing here?"

I tried to answer quickly. My voice was shaky, and I didn't want to confuse him any more than he was. "The bank needs you to pull over to a parking spot so they can talk to us."

He seemed confused, but he did appear to settle down as he said, "Well, why did they call me? We could have come over after work."

I wasn't sure what he was saying, his confusion was real, and I could see his emotional state had changed. He was back to the present and not even realizing what was going on.

The afternoon was a long one. I had Tim work in the warehouse while I went into my office and called the bank to thank them. I found out that they'd never called Tim, and they didn't know what they had done wrong. I assured them that he was confused, and it wasn't their fault.

As I hung up, Tim came in and asked what I was doing and when we were going home. He said he was tired, and if the bank hadn't called, we would have been home by now. It was only one o'clock, so I knew he was still thinking about years earlier, when he'd worked by himself. These days, it would be rare to get home before three.

Struggling to hold back my frustration and tears, I told Tim that we had to call the doctor, that something wasn't right.

I wasn't sure how he would handle me telling him this, but he took off his cap and rubbed his head from the top all the way to his chest. After a pause, he looked up at me and said, "You're right."

At that point, I knew it was time to make some decisions, mostly about our business, and this would affect every part of our lives.

Even though it was the hardest thing that I'd ever had to do, I needed to convince Tim that we must sell the business. While it was hard, I had already set things in motion some time ago. For the past several months, I had been talking to investors and some of our competitors, telling them in all honesty what was going on.

Most of the competitors had heard that there were problems, and it was amazing how compassionate and willing a couple of them were. We were well-liked and respected in the industry, and that was a great help.

The sale took place quickly, but not without arguments and frustrations as we both watched our dreams coming to an end. Many times, Tim accused me of having affairs with the people who were buying the business, or he would tell me I was ruining his life. I knew that this wasn't him talking, it was the disease, but it was still hard to go through all the emotional ups and downs, not only with Tim, but for my own part, as I was grieving the loss of the best husband in the world. I was now becoming a caregiver—to a man that sometimes didn't seem to like me much.

CHAPTER 7

onths went by. After the incident at the bank, life started to settle back down. It seemed that the medications were working, though the doses had to be adjusted frequently. I noticed that Tim was exhausted all the time. The doctors said he would adapt to the medications and he wouldn't be so tired. Then the neurologist added another pill to help with the exhaustion. This meant Tim was now up to fourteen total pills a day, taken at different times for different symptoms, costing us over a thousand dollars a month. I had to purchase a medicine reminder box. This wasn't only to help Tim remember, but it would allow me, at a glance, to make sure he had taken his meds on time and as needed.

We continued our doctors' visits as it seemed to help keep both of us grounded and focused. It was during one of our visits that I brought up with the neurologist a problem I had noticed over the past several months that was concerning to me.

It had actually become a daily argument. Tim and I had always loved to go out to the casino to have dinner and gamble a little—twenty or thirty dollars. We weren't big spenders, but it was a chance to get out, eat an inexpensive meal out, and be in a different world. For some time, I had stopped playing and started watching Tim play. We simply couldn't afford to do this.

When we closed up the business, Tim's business credit cards had a few thousand dollars from the casino on them. Our accountant pointed out the expenses—these weren't a business expense, and I wondered how long this had been going on. Tim had his own cards for business, and all of them were paid off every month. The accountant never said anything, he just did the books, and as he said, it was none of his business. It soon became his business when we closed our doors.

This was affecting our bottom line, and it didn't seem to bother Tim at all. He just wanted to go back to the casino.

In front of Tim, I explained to the doctor that I couldn't get him out of the casinos. I went on to tell how he would get angry if I wouldn't take him, and he was spending money and trying to hide it. As I made it clear that I felt he knew what he was doing, Tim abruptly interrupted me.

"You are taking away my life!" He was angry.

The doctor started to ask Tim questions, and yes, I was to blame. I hadn't wanted to rock the boat; I knew about the dementia problems, but I pushed them away because when Tim was at the casino, it was easier for me. He'd be happy for a few hours, and it seemed to be the only thing that was keeping him happy.

As the doctor continued talking, we found out that this problem—addiction—was caused by one of the medications. Worse, it had also advanced the dementia faster than had ever been documented. I was relieved to know we could stop the medication, but the experts didn't know if the worsening of the dementia would go away.

I was so angry with myself. I hadn't wanted to fight with Tim, so I'd given in over all those months, costing us thousands of dollars. All that time, it had been the medicine causing him these problems.

The doctor also mentioned that a new Neuro Wellness Center had opened up in our community. They specialized in Parkinson's, and they took walk-ins.

I was excited to find out more, but Tim wasn't too thrilled about it, saying, "I don't want to hang out with a bunch of old people."

I insisted we go and see what they had to offer. We didn't have anything better to do, after all. Even though Tim wanted to go to the casino, I knew that if we could get the right help and support, Tim would be open to it—or at least, that was what I was hoping for.

We went straight from the doctor's office to the wellness center. It was only a couple of miles up the road, but I had never heard Tim try to reject or complain as much as he did in those two miles, unless it was during a presidential campaign or going to a new doctor. As we pulled up to this beautifully designed and maintained heritage building, Tim said, "Oh look, all the old people must be giving them their money to make them better."

I snapped at him and said, "The center is upstairs—it's not the whole building!"

Tim said, "Well, guess we can't go up. You can't do stairs."

I answered abruptly, "There's an elevator."

Tim knew I wasn't giving in. He answered quietly, "I'm just joking with you."

As we got out of the van, we could see the elevator in the courtyard. As I started to walk to it, the smell of the flowers and fresh-cut grass filled the air. It was almost as if a calmness took over. I found myself taking deep breaths.

I looked at Tim, and he said, "This is really nice."

For the first time in a few months, I thought to myself, I was in the right place at the right time.

The elevator felt small, and I could see that Tim's tremor seemed a little worse. Looking at my watch, I realized he was past the time to take his medicine, but I stayed quiet. I wasn't going to let anything get in our way of trying to find some help.

We walked into a small reception area. A young man at the front desk looked up but didn't say anything. A beautiful woman came out of a small office area, and as she welcomed us, the look on her face said she was curious to know what we were doing there.

"Hi, I'm Annette. Welcome to our wellness center!" Her eyes sparkled as if we were the first people she'd spoken to all day. She pointed to the man at the front desk and added, "This is Ben, he's our exercise and rehabilitation trainer. What can we do for you?"

I introduced Tim and myself and told her our doctor had recommended that we come over and visit.

She politely asked if we were looking to help one of our parents, and I answered, "No, we're looking for my husband, Tim."

He hadn't said a word, but he tried to smile at her, saying, "What do you do here, just sit around looking pretty?"

I cringed inside. Annette had a work badge clipped to her shirt, and I could see that she was the manager of the facility.

She handled Tim with grace and a genuine smile. "No, I am the program manager here at our wellness center. We're privately owned and funded so we may offer complementary services to your current medical treatments and therapies for individuals and families who are affected by Parkinson's disease and other neurological conditions."

Tim answered in a sarcastic tone, "That's nice."

Annette looked at me. I knew Tim couldn't see my eyes, and I tried to shift them back and forth at her. For me, this was a new way of communicating, and I didn't like it, but it kept Tim calm to think he was controlling a situation. He had changed, and when he didn't get his way, he could be almost mean.

Annette looked at Ben, who was now standing uncomfortably in front of us as if protecting Annette. I could tell Tim was making them nervous. Annette asked Ben to show Tim around the facilities while she showed me the caregiver information.

"Caregiver," I heard Tim say as he was walking into the therapy room. "We take care of each other. She needs more help than I do."

I watched him walk into the other room and then had to look for a tissue as the tears started to flow. I had never let Tim know when I was frustrated or feeling overwhelmed, and he didn't like to see anyone cry, especially me.

I quickly explained to Annette that he was late for his dose of medication, and she quickly handed me a portable pill carrier for my purse and said to make sure I always had medicine, never to let him miss, and that some of his meds could cause emotional outbursts and other psychological problems. This was the first time anyone had said this to me. I realized that I had so much to learn, and now it definitely seemed that we had been guided to the right place at the right time.

After checking out the facilities, Tim was excited to "join up." However, while we were talking, an older woman came through the door, pushing her husband in a wheelchair. Tim's face turned almost gray, and his hazel eyes were larger than I had ever seen them before.

I wondered what he was thinking, but I quickly made an appointment to come back and have Tim evaluated. The service was free of charge, and they were so excited about us being there. I didn't think Annette or Ben had seen Tim's reaction to the man in the wheelchair.

Now, saying our goodbyes, I just hoped he wouldn't say anything obnoxious before we got out the door. As Tim and Ben shook hands, I could tell that Ben had made an impression, and Tim was leaving with confidence. Still, it seemed as if fear took over as we were leaving.

As we got into the elevator, Tim looked at me, and I was surprised to see his eyes had started to water. I asked him if he was okay, and his answer almost took my breath away.

"Do you think that will be me in a few years?"

As I tried to answer, a deep sigh came out first, and that caught me off guard. I finally said, "You know what the doctors told us. Everyone is different, and this program we just looked at is supposed to help." I just hoped he couldn't hear the doubt in my voice, because I didn't know, and there was no way of finding out.

CHAPTER 8

The next day, Tim woke up excited, and he talked about the center to the kids. They were aware of some of the struggles he was having, and they tried to be so supportive and loving. We were both grateful for the support, thinking that most teenagers would have hidden in their rooms. All this time, I had tried never to show any concern to anyone, including our family and friends. This had to be my secret—my strength. At that point, I didn't know I also needed the support of others. No, I was trying to be brave and handle everything on my own. I never knew how wrong I was.

No one had known that when we sold our business, we lost our health insurance. We'd bought it through our business, and the insurance company cancelled it on us when we closed. That was another mistake I had made, thinking we would be able to keep it. Now, every dime we were spending on meds and testing was coming out of our own pocket. Tim's meds came to over a thousand dollars a month, and I had to stop taking mine so we could afford his. The medical testing for every CAT scan, blood work, every doctor appointment added up to a sum in the thousands, and no companies would cover pre-existing conditions. As a result, we were going through any profit we'd made from selling our business in just a few months.

As the time to go to the wellness center approached, I was already drained, but Tim seemed more energetic than I had seen him for a while. "Hey, let's get going!" he said to me as I was locking up the house.

I nodded and with a smile said, "I'm ready if you are!" Off we went to the wellness center for his big evaluation, one that he was so proud to be doing.

When Tim walked in, it was with the personality of the man I fell in love with. He remembered their names and greeted them as if they were all the most important people in his life. I was so pleased that he was being positive about this, and I tried to think of how to ask him about the way he was feeling at that moment. I not only wanted to know, but I needed to, as I was wondering what was making him so happy at that moment.

As I sat in the reception area, Ben took Tim back for his evaluation, and Annette sat with me in the waiting area. At the moment, Tim and I were the only ones in the facility. Annette's compassion and genuine goodness were apparent from the first time we met. I sat there thinking how nice it was to have someone I could talk to while Tim was busy. This would be the first time since his diagnosis that I'd had a conversation with anyone without Tim by my side.

I must have been a little shaky myself, or just relieved to have a moment to think, when Annette asked me how I was. Their center wasn't only for the patient but for the family as well. She had received Tim's files from the doctor's office and had read in a side note that I had MS, another neurological disease they supported at the center.

I was taken back at first and quickly explained that I was there for Tim. I had my MS under control and didn't need help. I glanced over at Tim through the reception windows, and as I looked back at Annette, I realized I must have snapped at her. I seem to talk with my eyes more than my mouth, and this was something I was working on as Tim had learned to read me over the years. It seemed to me that now I had to try to have more patience. I had always believed in being kind to others, but lately, it seemed to be a struggle.

I apologized quickly, and all of a sudden, uncontrollable tears started streaming down my face. I couldn't believe it. What was going on? Why couldn't I control my emotions? And where is the tissue box? All of these thoughts were going through my mind at one time.

Annette stood and grabbed the tissues as if she'd read my mind. She said, "Holly, I am so sorry. I just wanted you to know that we are here to support you and Tim. Do you have any children?" That was one of the most gracious moments anyone had ever shared with me in my life.

After we'd spent over an hour getting to know each other, Annette looked at her watch and said she needed to make sure Ben was almost done as they had another evaluation coming in very soon. As she stood, Tim and Ben emerged from the workout area. The evaluation was done.

Tim smiled his new little smile and said, "I passed my test." I wondered what that meant. Ben started to speak, but Tim interrupted him and said, "I can come if I want."

I was happy to hear that but was still thinking to myself, *What does that mean?*

Ben glanced at Annette, and I worried to see a look of concern on his face as he handed her the evaluation. I said to them both, "I know that this is all new to us, but Tim is still trying to process everything, and I am just wondering if you can explain what our next step should be?"

Tim looked at me and said, "I'm coming back to exercise three or four days a week. They know what they are doing."

Annette looked at Ben and asked if Tim might need to have a little cool down on the exercise bike, and Ben answered quickly, "I was just going to suggest that."

Tim responded, "I am a little tired, and it's February."

I wasn't sure what February had to do with anything, but Ben told him that it would only be about five minutes, and that he shouldn't leave until he had cooled down. Then he escorted Tim back to the workout area.

As I stood there watching how happy Tim was, seeing his excitement about participating in the program, Annette tapped my shoulder and said, "Come over into my office." She explained that they had only been open for about a month. The facility was the creation of a local couple, Alan and Sheila, who herself has early onset Parkinson's. They had envisioned a place where others, sharing the same experiences she was going through in her journey, could come in here, even if they were shaking and twisting, no one would look twice at them or make them feel embarrassed by their situation. This was a place where people with Parkinson's and their families could socialize, develop a sense of community, and ultimately improve their quality of life. She said that Tim fit the criteria, but they were slightly concerned about his dementia, and did I feel he would be appropriate to be around others?

Wow, was all I could think. *What happened in his evaluation?* Annette's look of concern made me wonder out loud, "What did he do?"

It appeared that some of his remarks to Ben were concerning, and they wanted to know if this would be a problem.

Thinking of Tim's happy face when he'd said he was coming back, I knew I had to assure them that if Tim knew what was allowed, he would do just fine. In my heart, though, I knew I would have to find a way to tell him. He needed this program, and so did I. So, I promised to work with him and asked her to give us a chance.

She agreed with a smile that still had a tinge of concern. I reached out to hug her but then stopped and asked permission. We had always been hugging people, and silently trying to figure out what was appropriate, I said, "Tim and I both hug when we meet people."

She answered, "I love hugs, but Ben doesn't."

Now I knew that we might need to be more professional with Ben. That one statement would help me to coach Tim without him knowing I was coaching.

Over the next year, Tim's dementia seemed to stabilize, and he did well at the center. They followed the "Big and Loud" program, which encouraged big steps and louder voices, the two things that Parkinson's patients struggle with. This seemed to help Tim; having the support of others going through the same thing helped both of us—we weren't alone, there was a few people that were around our age and Ben worked well with Tim and got to know him. He helped me to see when Tim was struggling, which seemed to be a lot at this point. For example, a new symptom meant he was struggling to breathe when he was at the center—not all the time, but it was very noticeable.

CHAPTER 9

T he days seemed to get longer, and I struggled with finances. I remember the day Tim was approved for Social Security disability. While the money would help, it was the insurance for health care that I was relieved to finally have. Tim was struggling with so many new symptoms, and now he could finally get in to see a lung specialist to find out what was going on with his breathing, and he could possibly get reevaluated for his dementia, to see what was going on with that, even though I was pretty sure I knew.

To that point, every doctor we had talked to about his breathing thought Tim had to be a smoker, but he had never smoked a cigarette in his whole life. The lung specialist, thinking that possibly breathing the fumes from years of sanding and painting might be what was causing some of the problems, started to run more tests.

Tim was frustrated. He would make me and others uncomfortable, talking to medical personnel about subjects from breast sizes to telling them how "the doctor likes playing with my balls." I could tell his mental state was changing every day. He didn't hold back, and he didn't seem to care how uncomfortable he made others feel. I was always happy when we got home. For his part, he didn't think he was doing anything wrong as he was totally unaware of his inappropriate behavior.

A diagnosis with any form of dementia takes a lot of patience from the people around the person affected. Those who care for them and especially family members are being blamed for all the problems the patient is having, while people who aren't around every day still see the same person they always knew. Everyone loved Tim and simply couldn't see the dementia. They thought he was being funny, and they would laugh with him. This made it harder for us when we went out publicly with people that didn't know us. One day, I told him if he talked about his balls one more time, I would cut them off.

Of course, he thought that was funny, and he added it to his story.

We were very fortunate that we had found the wellness center. Not only did they help with rehabilitation, but when Tim and I were struggling financially, they helped with medication cost, and they also found a program to run Tim's DNA so we could find out more about his genes. Since he had other family members with Parkinson's, they thought it might be genetic. As a result, the Hollywood star who'd opened a foundation years ago paid for Tim's testing, a gift that was a real blessing.

Genetic testing for Parkinson's disease was very important at that time since not as much information was available then as there is today. PINK1 appears to be a rare cause of inherited Parkinson's disease. A small percentage of those who develop the condition at an early age appear to carry mutations in the PINK1 gene. Genetic testing is also done for the PARK7, SNCA, and LRRK2 genes. Tim's testing came back showing no affected genes that were associated with Parkinson's, and so we knew that it was something in his environment. Again, this led us back to his childhood home, where so many other people had neurological problems, and some had even died from many forms of cancer.

Even though this was devastating to find out, it was also a relief to know that the children wouldn't have to worry about Parkinson's being inherited from a family gene. The children were happy to know this, and we as a family were so grateful for all the testing that was a part of this program. As a kind of bonus, we even found out more about Tim's health and the things that we should be watching out for.

CHAPTER 10

Time seemed to go by quickly. My family, especially my mom, wanted to find a way to spend time together as a family and just try to enjoy ourselves. My grandfather had passed away, and she had inherited a little bit of money. She had enjoyed a cruise she'd taken with my brother to Europe. It had been such a special time for her that she wanted to go again, and Alaska was the next adventure she wanted to take.

My mom and her husband, "Papa," approached my two sisters, Tim, and myself about going on a cruise to Alaska. She had heard about this vacation for years and felt that the six of us could have time to spend together, a wonderful vacation—no children, just the six of us enjoying time together.

I was excited, and we all started working on getting this trip together, but at home, Tim was reluctant, almost scared. This surprised me because he was happy and excited in front of my mom, but to me, he showed fear and anxiety that was hard for me to understand. Tim was always able to tell everyone how "awesome" things were, but he'd get frustrated when we got home. He'd even blame me when he thought people were treating him differently.

Sometimes he'd talk to the kids when he didn't think I was listening, and he would tell them I was changing. He'd say I was making things hard on him. I never told the kids about the conversations I heard because I never wanted them to feel like they were stuck in between us. At this point, the children weren't even aware of the dementia; they just thought it was part of the Parkinson's. I never corrected them. We had enough going on in our lives.

It was important to me that this trip would be a memorable one for everyone, including Tim. I knew he'd enjoy it. I also knew I would never be able to tell anyone what we were going through at home. I didn't want anyone to feel badly because everyone was excited about going. We only needed to get our passports and get ready. As neither of us had a passport, this would be our first step because we would need one to book the trip.

As we sat in the passport office, Tim was nervous, and his tremors and speech were frightening. I knew that he'd had his medication, so I wasn't sure what was going on. We waited for about ten minutes before we were called up to the window. Tim looked at the woman and said, "So this is the place where she signs me up to get rid of me."

The woman looked up from behind her reading glasses and said, "Are you here for a passport?"

I quickly said yes and grabbed Tim's hand to lead him to the chair. He was rubbing the brim of his cap, and I knew he wasn't trusting the situation.

I handed our birth certificates and identification to her and quickly started to ask questions about why it was necessary to have passports to travel to Alaska. I was trying to keep Tim from getting upset or saying something that would get us thrown out of the office. As she spoke, she looked at me as if I was asking too many questions. I said rather sharply, "My husband has Parkinson's, and we are just curious."

When she finally caught on, she stood up and went to the back of her office, which gave me time to calm Tim down and explain to him that we had to have a passport. I wasn't dropping him off or leaving him anywhere; we were all going together as a family.

He looked up at me and said, "Yeah, right—if your mom doesn't get rid of us in Alaska."

The woman came back and finished our applications. Now I knew that his dementia and paranoia were worse, and I realized I had been looking past so many things. I knew I needed help, but I didn't know how to go about it.

The application process only took a few minutes, but I was never so happy to get out of a building in my life. I held Tim's hand as we left and told him if he didn't want to go, we wouldn't.

He stopped, pulled his hand away, and said, "I am not going to be the one to blame for ruining your mom's trip."

I knew I would never be able to tell my family what we were going through. Everyone saw Tim as a fun-loving guy who would do anything in the world for anyone, the man every woman dreams of. No one knew of the man he had become, the fears and paranoia we were living with every day. To be honest, I didn't want either of us to be judged or looked at differently as I knew this could worsen Tim's aggression and paranoia. He would blame me for things going wrong. If someone else even looked at me wrong, I would hear about it for days.

We finally got the trip booked after weeks of me reassuring Tim that everything would be okay and promising him it would be the best time of his life. We would eat, drink, and spend time together—no doctors, no problems, just fun. We would finally be able to board the cruise ship with anticipation and excitement.

Even though we had encountered typical travel problems before when we'd traveled, this trip was difficult for me. It wasn't the same as our monthly visits to Las Vegas to visit his father in a long-term care facility. There, I knew how he would react. This was on a ship in the middle of the ocean, and out of thousands of people, I would be the only one who knew about his dementia and his paranoia. I could only hope it wouldn't get out of control.

Papa was sick most of the time. He had problems with his medications, and that kept the rest of the family focused on something else. That meant I could just smile and hold Tim's hand and enjoy being with my family, and it was all worth it. It was a vacation full of memories that will last forever, at least for me. I didn't know how long Tim would remember, or if he would even remember by the time we got home. The main thing was that my mom was happy, and she got her wish to have a vacation with her daughters.

I will always be grateful for this vacation as this would be one of the last times that Tim and I would truly enjoy ourselves. I also knew when I got home that it was time for me to get more information about how Parkinson's changes, especially the emotional state of the people who are affected by it. Mostly, I had to figure out how I was going to start telling others about the dementia—without upsetting Tim.

When I'd worked at the long-term care facility, I had taken many classes and earned certifications for dealing with all types of age-related problems, including dementia. That helped me understand what was going on, but I needed more. I still had a child at home, and four others that we saw almost every week, and they knew something wasn't right. As for his whole family, who lived out of state, they knew nothing except about the Parkinson's, even though we regularly traveled to Las Vegas to visit his father. In addition, Tim had a complete medical and personal power of attorney for his father. So, I knew the day the ship docked that things would never be the same.

CHAPTER 11

As weeks and even months went by, my relationship with Tim became that of a caregiver instead of a wife. After returning from the cruise, I met with doctors and psychologists referred by the wellness center. I found out that there was nothing I could do, other than being supportive and keeping Tim positive and active. This would also be the only thing I could do for the dementia. They told me about programs and long-term care facilities where he could be admitted, but that was not something I was interested in. I knew I could do it on my own, even though by now, others had started to notice the changes in Tim. I wanted him to be at home with me and the kids, and although I had only told our children and my parents about the dementia, I still hadn't told Tim's family. While he was legally responsible for all the decisions for his father, I knew that his father was safe and well taken care of.

Our sister-in-law worked at the facility where Tim's dad lived, and I trusted her. Every month, Tim still insisted on going to visit his dad and family in Las Vegas. It was only a five-hour drive. The trip gave Tim something to look forward to. We'd done this for years, and it was a part of Tim's "schedule" that helped him feel as if life was normal. As I knew his dad was safe, I didn't tell anyone about the dementia. When Tim was abrupt and sometimes aggressive, I just told everyone that it was the Parkinson's, that he was having a bad day. One time, he even told me, "You might as well get me a bed in this place."

On some trips, it was tempting.

The youngest child was now the only one at home, and she had become Tim's main focus. This was hard for her, but she never complained, and the closeness and support she showed her father were inspiring. I made sure he could participate in everything from her raising pigs for the FFA (Future Farmers of America) to softball games. I'd call and see if I could get him on as a coach. These were exhausting days, but I'd learned that the busier I kept Tim, the more focused he was.

Some days, he'd tell me that he would do it just to please "your boyfriend" or "your lover." Tim was totally convinced that I was having an affair with our daughter's teacher because I spent so much time talking to him. Ironically, he forgot he was right there with me every time the teacher and I talked. The paranoia sometimes was scary, and I would continue to hear him tell the children stories about what he imagined was happening. I just kept praying that they knew how much I loved their dad. His well-being was all that mattered, so I would never confront Tim; instead, I made sure he was always "right," no matter how wrong I knew he was.

I had always been a spiritual person, and at this point, I needed all the support I could get. I had experienced many different things in my life. I had been blessed with a gift of true spiritual connection. I got messages from people who had passed and was even able to know what someone was going through in their life by way of messages from the spirits around those people.

This spiritual connection started when I was very young. When I would "talk" to my spirits, my parents would tell people I had an active imagination, that I should be in the movies. They called me a "liar" and a "storyteller." This stayed with me, and I hid my spiritual connection from my family as I learned from a young age that no one would ever believe me. But I knew that I was being protected by these spirits, and they would make sure I knew I had a gift and to cherish it.

Tim was aware of this from the first day we met. I'd asked him about his mother and told him that she was with him. The message from her was direct and loving. Because I was able to tell him her name, he knew I wasn't playing with him. He was the first person in my life that supported my gift and truly loved it when I would talk to complete strangers and give them a message from a loved one that had passed. Some people would say I was a medium—I would say a messenger, as we all have this gift. Some use it, but others don't even know they have it, and some know they have it but are afraid of it.

It was taking more energy to care for Tim. With the stresses I was incurring and everything that had been going on, it seemed I was only picking up on major things and ignoring some of them. Tim pushed me about why I hadn't been giving any messages. He wanted to know what his mom was telling me about him, and this became one of his obsessions. I tried to turn it off so he wouldn't be so focused on wanting and needing messages. I told him I wasn't getting anything, even though I knew that we had more spirits around us in the house. Our lights flickered off and on, the ceiling fan changed speeds, or the car radio turned itself up. I knew that they were wanting to be heard.

Tim loved it. When it happened, he'd say, "They're back" in a weird voice, but I would answer, "They're just saying hi."

CHAPTER 12

We had continued our trips to visit with Tim's dad and family, but now the Parkinson's was making it difficult for Tim to travel. His body would lock up, and that was very painful for him, so we started going every few weeks. I would make sure we got there a day before we had to see anyone so Tim would be emotionally and physically rested. After a drive, his paranoia and aggression were overwhelming, but I could take him to the casino in the hotel where we were staying, and it would be like the old Tim was back, happy and content. That way, by the time we saw everyone, he would seem normal—or at least normal for Tim.

Since we weren't working, we could stay a little longer on these trips. We started taking our youngest daughter and her friends for birthday celebrations, New Year's, anything so that we could be together. As a bonus, when Tim was happy and concentrating on the girls, he wasn't as aggressive. Furthermore, the paranoia was more prevalent when we weren't following a schedule the way he thought we should.

Early in June 2012, Tim began to tell me that his mother was "visiting" him. I started a detailed journal of this as I knew his mind was open to receive messages. Because he believed it could happen and would say it out loud all the time, I wanted to document what was going on.

We had just had a huge sixteenth birthday party for our daughter, and I was exhausted, but Tim was very active and focused. He was insistent that I needed to focus on the fact that his mother was in the house. He said she was happy and thrilled. Our youngest had been only a baby when she'd passed away, and Tim was excited that she was sharing this time with us.

I knew I was in for a long night. When Tim got like this, I was afraid he might try to drive himself some place or go fishing in the middle of the night. I went and got myself a cup of green tea, and as I was reaching for the cup, the lights in the kitchen started to flicker off and on. Tim got really excited and anxious. I went to him, hugged him, and said, "Yes, your mom is here." I knew it was his mom. I could smell her perfume, and I asked if she was there. My problem is that when it comes to my own life, I cannot receive messages. I guess that's part of my own journey.

I kept wondering what was going on. Not only was Tim's mom in the house, but it was like Grand Central Station. I guess that since I was focusing, the spirits had a lot to share, but Tim only picked up on his mom's spirit. I knew that spirits are always there when someone passes away, and I began to worry. Was Tim worse than I thought? Was his mom there to escort him "Home"?

All of a sudden, a calmness came over me. No, she wasn't there to escort him to heaven, she was there to help. My prayers had been answered. Tim would now be focusing on this spiritual journey, and this would help me keep him calm.

In that moment, he said to me, "My mom hates when I treat you bad."

I thought to myself, *I do, too!*

Over the next few weeks, I don't think Tim slept longer than forty-five minutes at a time. When we talked to the doctor about it, Tim told him, in answer to the doctor's questions, about his mother and her visits. I watched the doctor's eyes get big, and you could see from his face that he was nervous. He couldn't believe what he was hearing, and he was convinced that it was time for Tim to be admitted to a hospital because the paranoia and delusions were out of control.

I burst out laughing. I didn't know if he thought I should also be admitted, but I explained to him the spiritual awareness that Tim had found. Even though it might not be normal, it wasn't psychotic. I also told him that if I felt there was a problem, I would let him know.

He was far from being convinced, not only did he have a patient who believed in spiritual intervention, but the wife believed even more. He wrote a prescription for a strong sleep aid, and off we went.

I was still giggling inside my mind. Sometimes, the narrow-mindedness of others surprised me. If you believe in God, then why wouldn't you believe in angels and that the spirits of those that have passed could be in the realm of the world we live in?

I didn't know at the time of this doctor visit that such "help" might not be good for a person suffering with dementia and paranoia. I'd always felt that spiritual guidance was a true blessing.

It was a struggle. Tim was focused on trying to communicate with his mother. It became part of an obsessed way of thinking for him, and he wanted me to acknowledge everything he was hearing.

One night, he woke me up at two in the morning and said, "Your dad is with my mom."

I sat straight up in the bed and thought, *Well, how did he get there?* We had just seen him in Las Vegas, and I had talked to him on the phone a couple of days before.

"He's dead, he passed away, or at least, I think that's what she's saying."

I could feel my heart stop beating for a moment, and then I started to ask him questions. I wasn't going to call my father in the middle of the night. His words, when he'd said, "that's what I think she is saying," kept going through my head. *Don't panic, Holly! You aren't feeling your dad!* I always knew when someone in my life was sick or had passed away; this was a part of my "gift."

But Tim was insistent, and we spent the next few hours trying to figure out what he was hearing. I called the nursing home at the facility where his father was—he was fine, but that made Tim believe more strongly that it was my dad.

I wasn't going to start calling anyone in the middle of the night, but then Tim started crying, and he said, "I know I am hearing something about Dad, and we need to find out!"

I was grateful our youngest had been spending the night with a friend. This wasn't something I would have wanted anyone to see; this was severe anxiety with the paranoia, and since he hadn't been sleeping, his Parkinson's symptoms were severe.

In the morning, Tim was scheduled for one of his three weekly exercise classes at the wellness center. He didn't want to go until I'd talked to my dad. Honestly, I was a little afraid to call. Had he passed away in the middle of the night? Was Tim, right? But I knew my dad would never answer his phone before ten, so I didn't want to panic myself any more than I had been all night. I'm close to my dad, and I would be devastated if something happened and we didn't connect spiritually if he passed.

At about 9:15 a.m., Tim was in class, but he kept watching me through the window. As she did every time we were there, Annette came over, but this time, she said, "Holly, you look terrible."

I started to cry, not thinking that Tim might be able to see me, and he ran out of the class, saying, "Are you okay? Is your dad dead?"

I quickly answered him. "I haven't called yet."

He stomped off back to his class, glaring at me through the window. I pretended not to see him. I smiled at Annette and told her I would talk to her later. She walked back to her office. Within a minute, I had a text message from her asking if I was okay. I texted back that I was fine. I explained a little to her via text. Then, at almost 9:30, a calming feeling came over me.

This was a sense of relief. Even though I hadn't called yet, I knew my dad was fine. I showed my phone to Tim as I got up to let him know I was going to call. Then I walked out of the building. I dialed, and at the other end, my dad said, "You're calling early—how did you know I was up?"

I said, "I'm just checking in with you. I had a rough night, and I was worried about you!" I explained a small portion of what had happened and ended the conversation with "I am glad you're okay!"

He answered, "When it *is* my time, I will check in with you."

Tim was happy to find out that my dad was alive and well, but now he was worried about what his mother was trying to say to him. I told him it takes a while to understand and communicate with spirits, but when the message was strong enough, he would understand.

CHAPTER 13

Within a six-week span, Tim's obsessive behavior was noticeable to everyone he talked to. He told them about his mother and how she was talking to him, saying that she needed him to do something, and he was having problems understanding. So many of our friends and family were worried, especially his family in Las Vegas, and his brother voiced concerns that maybe Tim's medication was giving him hallucinations. This upset Tim so much that he stopped talking to his brother. I don't think his brother ever caught on because if he called, I would tell him Tim was resting. This only lasted a couple of weeks, and as long as Tim didn't have to talk, he was okay.

One night, Tim woke me up, turned on the bedroom light, and said, "Get dressed, we have to go."

I could barely focus, but I could tell he was agitated and seemed very confused. As I tried to calm him, he started to explain. "My mom wants me to go get my dad out of the nursing home and bring him back here. We need to go." I sat straight up in bed and realized my headache had just gotten worse. Tim was putting his shoes on, and he had the keys in his hands. He was trying to leave to go pick up his dad.

When I was able to focus, I realized he wasn't having a "dementia moment"; he had finally understood what his mother was trying to communicate to him. I was amazed—and frightened. How was I going to tell him that we couldn't do this when I knew, the minute he'd said it, he'd gotten the message right. Yes, his mother wanted us to go get his wheelchair-bound father and bring him to Arizona. This was going to be a struggle, not only for me, but what if his dad didn't want to come? We had talked to him about it a few times, and he was scared of traveling.

I calmed Tim down and tried to explain to him that his power of attorney didn't give him the right to pull his dad out of a long-term care facility. He fought me on this, and I had to explain that even though we had been paying cash, by law, we had to have a plan, a place for him to stay, caregivers and doctors willing to take over his care, and least of all, transportation. This wasn't going to be easy. Although I knew I could do it—I had done this for so many families—was my health ready to add another person needing care to our home? Not a lot of money was left in his father's account; he was within weeks of the state taking over his care. We had sold his house, and we had spent almost every dime on the facility and his dad's care over the years he was there. If we were going to do this, it would be at our expense, and I was worried. I knew his Social Security was enough to pay to get some help every month. I had contacts with doctors who did house calls, and caregivers who could help bathe and take care of him, but with the behavioral problems I was having with Tim, could I do it?

I tried for almost a week to talk Tim out of this, but in my heart, I knew there was a reason we were supposed to get Tim's dad out of the facility. Now I knew why, years ago, I had taken a job in a long-term care facility. It was for this moment: I had to help Tim, and I knew we couldn't let anyone in Nevada know until the day we got there what we were doing. If we had all the right paperwork, permissions, and transportation, they couldn't stop us.

It took me six days to get everything together, and the whole time it was a fight to keep Tim calm, going over and over what we had to do. He didn't understand the legalities or the consequences. Our biggest expense would be the transportation. An ambulance was going to cost us thousands, and we didn't have that. Then, one day, I found a van rental with a lift gate and transport safety features, and I knew this was going to happen. However, my headache just seemed to be getting worse. I knew I had to get this done, and as quickly as I could.

I knew there were going to be problems, especially with the facility, as well as my sister-in-law, Tim's brother's wife. She had been so good to Dad over the years that I was afraid she'd think we didn't appreciate everything she'd done. The night before we were to leave, we tried to call her, but they weren't home. This wasn't something we would leave on an answering machine for them to hear when only a few hours later, we'd be there.

On that five-hour drive, I explained to Tim that if he lost his temper or we couldn't get his dad to agree, this would be over. I wanted to be at the facility before any of the administration got in so we could explain to Dad what was going on and that we wanted him to come with us to Arizona. I was glad we did because he thought we were joking. As he sat there in his bed, waiting for his breakfast, he asked, "Are you going to bring me breakfast in bed every morning?"

I took out my cell phone. The plan was about to unfold.

I started with pictures of his room. We had turned a family room off the kitchen into a private suite with an extended-size hospital bed as Tim's dad, Jim, was over 300 lbs. I showed him the sitting area for visitors, the large-screen TV, and the fireplace. He was starting to smile.

The girl with his breakfast came in, and he told her, "I'm going to Arizona!"

Unfortunately, Tim added, "And no one can stop us."

I knew I had to move quickly. This facility was a small but nicely appointed place, and this girl knew our sister-in-law, so she would be back to Jim's room very soon.

I continued to show Jim the rest of his suite, the Hoyer lift in his room to help lift him in and out of bed, and even a picture of the caregiver we'd hired. I showed him a receipt to prove she was working for us and the most important piece of paper, a release from the facility's care from a doctor who would be taking over Jim's health-care needs. This, with Tim's power of attorney, should do it. This was everything that I knew I'd need to get him released.

Now the big decision time came. It was up to Jim. He said, "I can't ride in a car. How am going to get there?"

I pulled back the curtains to his window. I had purposely parked the transport van so he could see it from his room.

He smiled and looked at Tim. "Do you want me to come?"

Tim said, "Yes, and so does Mom."

I thought, *Oh no! Let's not do this.* I had told him not to bring it up, but he was going to do it his way, and I couldn't say anything.

For the first time, I was glad that we hadn't told the family about the dementia because that could have revoked his power of attorney. However, I was the second one named on everything. Jim trusted me, and if anything happened to Tim, I was to take care of everything for Jim. This had been a touchy situation with Tim's brothers and sisters-in-law, and I didn't want to be the one forcing anything. I love this family. They had all helped change my life over the twelve years I'd been a part of their family.

It was a hard day, but we knew we had to leave so we could drive back to Arizona and get Jim settled. The facility tried every way they could to stop us, but I had everything I needed. Over the years that Jim was there, we had paid out almost three hundred thousand dollars, and if Jim had stayed and let the state take over his care, they would have doubled what we were paying them monthly. I knew, because I had been in this situation where I had worked, that you never wanted to let someone go out the door, especially after making so much money from them.

The trip home was long. Jim hadn't been out of the facility except to do activities with the other patients. He was excited, and he couldn't wait to get home so he and Tim could fish off the deck in our back yard every night. As we drove into the driveway, I could feel my body trembling. This had been emotionally and physically hard on me, and now I had two men to take care of. Yes, I'd have help with the physical part, but emotionally, each of them needed to be supported differently. In addition, my father-in-law had a problem controlling his mouth, so now I'd have to be listening and correcting not just Tim but also his father all the time.

The kids were so happy to see their grandfather. Even though it was the hottest time of the year, August, they would try to come and fish and spend time with him. Jim was so happy. He told Tim and me that when he got sick at the nursing home, they kept taking him to the hospital even though he told them he didn't want to go. He didn't want to do that anymore. He also liked the doctor that came to our home. He said that if he was dying, he would rather do it at home, and he would refuse to be taken to the hospital. I tried to tell him he wasn't dying, that if he had a heart attack, I would have to call 911.

He said in answer to this, "I will kill you," and even though I knew he would never do that, I knew he was serious. I realized we had to do something because he had to have this in writing to prove these were his wishes.

That evening, when Tim and I went to our room, I had to explain to Tim that we couldn't make his dad do something he didn't want to do. He would have to sign a "Do Not Resuscitate" or DNR, and I'd have to call in someone else to take care of that. We couldn't be responsible for this decision.

At first, Tim said, "No, he needs to go to the hospital," but after three days of fighting with his father, he gave in.

When he left the room, frustrated, Jim asked me what was wrong with his son. He had noticed changes, and he didn't like that. I finally told Jim the whole story. As he was lying in the bed, he'd been watching and listening to how Tim was acting. I couldn't hide it. Over the six days that had gone by since we'd brought Jim home, Tim had shown a huge decline in his mental health.

Jim told me that he was frightened by what he saw. While he was very happy to be with us, he didn't want me to tell the rest of the family because he didn't want to go back to the facility. I tried to reassure him that all would be okay and that when Tim got enough rest, he'd be different. In the back of my mind, I was thinking I really didn't know that. Had I gotten myself in so deep that I would be regretful? My gut was telling me we had done the right thing, but my heart was aching from the pain I was feeling.

The doctor we'd hired to take care of Jim in our home came to the house to verify and notarize the DNR, but he told Jim, "You're going to be just fine."

Jim countered him, saying, "Maybe not."

I got the kind of goosebumps that always told me something was going on. Jim was sure he wouldn't be around for very long, and that was why he'd agreed to come to Arizona.

The doctor tried to convince Jim that all was good.

Jim didn't feel that way. He insisted on calling friends and family, and he spent time over the next couple of weeks trying to make amends for past mistakes and problems that he'd had. It really bothered Tim that his dad kept thinking he was dying, when Tim had brought him home because his mother had told him to.

Tim was aware of what his father was doing, and now he was obsessively questioning why he hadn't gotten any more messages from his mom. Was his dad dying? Why had he gotten the message to bring Jim to Arizona?

He was emotional, and some of the time, he seemed jealous because I had to spend time with his father. I had put a monitor in the room with Jim, in case, when we went to bed at night, he needed anything. He would just have to speak, which he did two to three times a night, and it would wake me. As a result, exhausted and not feeling well, I was now concerned that this might have been a mistake.

Even though I kept Tim's schedule and kept up all his classes, made sure Jim was taken care of and the house was in order, our youngest child was starting to struggle as I didn't seem to have as much time for her. This devastated me. It was truly a situation I had to change. We needed more quality time as a family, without talking about someone being sick or her grandfather talking about dying.

When we were only ten days into our new adventure, I started to make changes that I knew would help everyone—including me. I put together some guidelines of helpful things for the family to read and to help understand more about dementia because now we had two people with different levels, though Tim was far worse than his father. The main thing I wanted everyone to know was to keep calm and try to sit or stand still when talking to either of them. I asked everyone to avoid speaking sharply or raising their voices because people with dementia may respond with impatience or even aggression if they can't find the right words to express what they mean. I had found out from my own experience: at first, I would try to answer for my husband, thinking I was helping, but it only made the situation worse. Patience was very important, and our whole family needed to work on this.

I reminded everyone that if they were struggling to understand a situation—which seemed to be almost every person who came to visit—they should try asking Tim or Jim if they could explain something in a different way. Listening for clues and paying attention to their body language could really help. Some of the visitors would be able to interpret what Tim or Jim was saying, but they needed to make sure to confirm that they understood the situation. This was crucial. A wrong interpretation could lead to undue agitation, and this could and sometimes did lead to an explosive reaction.

CHAPTER 14

We have always been a very emotional and huggy-type family. We hug each other when we see each other, when we're leaving, and even to congratulate each other. Showing care and affection for our loved ones was a must. I had learned that maintaining physical contact throughout the stages of any life-altering illness is important, not only for them, but for you. A hug can make us all feel better, and hugging is something I did numerous times a day.

Sometimes Jim wasn't open to this, so I would at least touch his arm or hold his hand for a minute. He wasn't used to that as no touching had ever been allowed at the facility. Tim, on the other hand, would take as many hugs as he could get.

The days were getting easier. As Tim and his dad spent time fishing, having lunch, and watching sports together, I finally knew we had made the right decision. I had gotten a schedule down that seemed to work for all of us. Since finding out about Tim, Jim was being more careful about what he said, and he tried very hard to keep calm. He had seen too many emotional outbursts in the three weeks he had been here, and this seemed to make him more compassionate and understanding. I wondered how he felt, watching his son going through this. Many times, I could see worry in his eyes.

One morning, a few days later, I was in the kitchen making breakfast. As Jim was talking to me from the other room, I could hear his words slur a little. I thought maybe he was choking on some food—he would always try to sneak some candy at different times of the day—but then it seemed to get worse. I rushed into his room and saw that his face looked crooked. The last time I had seen something like that, it was a stroke. I ran to the phone to call 911. When my eyes fell on the bright orange paper next to phone—DNR—my heart missed a beat, and I picked up the phone and called the doctor.

Luckily, the doctor was down the road at the hospital, so it didn't take him too much time to get there. I had given Jim two aspirins, like the doctor had told me to do, and Jim seemed to be okay. He was slurring his words, but everything else seemed okay. The doctor arrived, and after examining Jim, he knew that Jim had suffered a small stroke, but the aspirin was hopefully helping. He talked to Jim, telling him that a CT scan could verify it.

Jim refused to go to the hospital.

As I asked him over and over, Tim started to throw a fit, saying, "My dad said no. Leave him alone."

All I could think was that if he'd been at the facility, they would have made him go. This was Jim's wish, however, so I needed to understand and be patient. It was hard to do, but the doctor reassured me that everything seemed to be okay.

That's when I realized there had to be a reason that Jim was so adamant. Maybe he was ready to go. I kept thinking, *He is seventy-nine and has been stuck in a bed for over six years!* It was as if *I* was finally understanding.

As I calmed down, I felt the presence of Marine, Tim's mom. She was here, and this was her reason to get Jim to Arizona. Maybe it was time for him to be with her. If he'd stayed in the facility, this couldn't happen.

Before the doctor left, he wrote an order for hospice to come and evaluate Jim. Since his DNR had already been completed, it was only a little paperwork. They tried to reassure us that Jim appeared to be fine. They mentioned that they'd had patients on hospice for up to two years with qualifying conditions, but it all sounded so final to me. We'd just gotten Jim home, and now he was agreeing to be put on hospice. I had always respected the hospice program and even recommended it to so many of the family members I had worked with, but this just seemed to be happening so fast.

The next day, after talking with both Jim and Tim, we made the decision to call all the family, ours and the out-of-towners, and fill everyone in on what was going on. The brother and sisters-in-law were very upset, saying that if he was there, he wouldn't be on hospice. They even stated that the drive had been too hard on him, and this was all our fault.

Unfortunately, I knew I also had to tell them about Tim, that he had been struggling with dementia. He didn't need to be blamed for anything, and they shouldn't make him feel any worse than he already did.

The phone calls from the family continued, and Tim's frustration was very hard to control. I was really worried about Tim, and I tried to make things better for him: we would play cards, or go fishing, anything to keep his mind off the way he was feeling. The biggest comfort Tim felt was that his mother, Marine, was with us, and he felt her love and support.

In less than a week, we lost Jim. He went very quietly. Our oldest daughter, Tim, and I were by his side. Although it was very peaceful, Tim had problems coping. Even though he was glad he'd helped his dad, he was taking a lot of blame on himself.

This affected him emotionally and physically. He was struggling with wanting to go to his classes at the wellness center, and he now had little control over his feelings. When he was upset, he would show it; when he was sad, he would cry—sometimes uncontrollably, for hours. The doctors started to warn me that these symptoms could be permanent, and I needed to be as supportive as I could. They said that people with dementia cannot process grief like others do.

The next few weeks continued to be emotional as we had to take care of the funeral arrangements, including shipping Jim's body to Utah, his final resting place. As we were working on this, Tim would receive calls. Although he'd try to understand what everyone was wanting from him, he'd get angry. If I tried to help, he would get very frustrated. "This is my father, and I will make the decisions!"

To make matters worse, the funeral home was charging us every time someone changed their minds—and so many family members were calling them.

Tim was confused, and his paranoia was working overtime. He thought everyone was against him.

I had worried about it, so behind Tim's back, I went to the funeral home. I took all our paperwork and explained that Tim was the only one to make decisions, that no one else was to allowed to change or make any decisions. After explaining to the funeral home that Tim and I were the only ones that had a power of attorney, things went smoother. At last, Tim had a chance to feel like he was making these decisions, and this helped keep him calm.

Before we were going to leave for Utah, I needed to get Tim in to see his doctor. For one thing, I needed to get some anxiety medication for him as well as something to help him sleep. I was worried about how he would react when we were driving and what others would say to him when we got there.

Our drive to Utah went better than expected. The whole family was there. My mom drove with us to Utah, and Tim had always looked to her like she was his own mother. This would be the first time that my mom would spend an extended amount of time with Tim, and I worried about how she would feel when she knew what was going on with Tim's emotional health.

She was wonderful and helped us get through a very hard time. When Tim got upset, she stepped in, being the mom he needed. It was as if he was listening to her like a child would listen to its mother. I was truly grateful and glad she was with us. Somehow, I knew that this trip, even though it was hard on the whole family, would help us get through some hard times that would be coming for us down the road.

CHAPTER 15

Settling back into our daily routine had become a struggle. Our adult children didn't visit as frequently as they once had. Tim was affected by this, and his paranoia made him believe that they didn't love him like they used to. His confidence in himself and others no longer existed.

My heart ached. I felt lost and didn't know how to help. I just tried to stay calm and patient. I remember looking at the clock all day, waiting for night to come so we could go to bed to get away from the emotional ups and downs of the day. Even though sleep didn't come as easily as I wanted, just resting in bed would help relax me, giving me time to meditate and get centered to start the next day.

Even though we knew others at the wellness center who were having great marital relations—and some of them were a lot older then we were—sex wasn't something either of us showed any interest in. We would tease each other, hug and hold each other at night, but sex had become a distant memory of what our lives had been before.

Now I wanted to be held. However, after the verbal and constant emotional embarrassment, no matter how many times I tried to communicate this, it seemed that Tim always went back to blaming me for all the problems we were having. Some days, I felt as if I couldn't do anything right, but I knew I couldn't get upset or show emotion as this would make it even more difficult for the whole family.

The change in Tim's behavior and his troubles with reasoning and confusion made his alertness vary significantly from one time of day to another or from one day to the next. I'd known that this would happen, and it had. It was so hard to understand why it was happening so quickly. I wondered if the emotion of losing his father had sped the progression in his changes.

Sometimes, when others talked to me, they would say, "Tim worships you. He loves you so much." No one knew the struggles we were having in the bedroom. While some could see the changes, it was at that time that I knew we both had built up a wall around our sex life, and it just wasn't going to happen. Dementia not only affected Tim, but it also affected the way I reacted to him.

As I woke every morning, my nightmare seemed to follow me through the day. Life wasn't what I'd thought it would be, and all the dreams of a happily-ever-after didn't seem to exist. I was exhausted—and scared. I just didn't know how I would make it through each day.

But I did. Just like so many others do every day, I prayed and kept the faith that I was doing the right thing for Tim and our family. Faith was all I had left, and I needed to keep it to keep going.

We continued to go to wellness classes. Tim and our youngest were my main focus. As the days continued, Tim was struggling. The only thing he wanted to do was lie down and watch sports or spend time with our youngest daughter. They were getting closer every day, and I worried about how he would handle it when she graduated from high school and went off to college. I thought about this every night, worrying about what would happen, but then something would bring me back to the problems of the day, and I would have to worry about the future later, one day at a time.

CHAPTER 16

Our youngest daughter shared so much in common with her father, and this helped Tim get through his days. He had been in the Future Farmers of America, FFA, in high school, and she was following in his footsteps. Her agriculture teacher was always looking for volunteers to help with the program. Tim had been raised on a pig farm, so I encouraged him to talk to the teacher. Tim could talk about his younger days without a problem, and he could be very helpful, and I loved marketing and sales. The teacher agreed to let us help.

We both started spending time at the school, working with the students and coaching them on different aspects of agriculture experiences and leadership skills to help with testing and competitions. Tim was so happy to have something to look forward to, and three years in a row, our youngest had raised a pig. Tim focused on helping her to take care of pigs, and he loved spending time with his daughter.

Because this gave Tim so much to look forward to, and he was staying busy at the school and the wellness center, I've always felt that this helped him get over the death of his father. He was able to focus on his own health, and even though the doctors reminded me monthly that Tim wasn't getting better, it seemed to me that he was happy and content. Even when his paranoia surfaced, it didn't last as long, especially when he was around the kids.

We spent many afternoons planning fun things to do with our first grandson, and we were expecting a second grandchild soon. Tim joked that at fifty-three, not only did he feel old having two grandchildren, but his body and mind were around eighty years old. I always smiled, but deep inside, I felt bad. I wondered how long he would be able to spend with his grandchildren and if he would forget the times he was having with them.

Life was definitely better than it had been for a long time. Tim's medication controlled his tremors and some of the dementia and para- noia problems. He could hold a conversation a little longer before losing track of what he was doing, and as he continued his exercise program, his stability and strength also improved. The breathing prob- lems had stayed the same, but his inhaler helped those symptoms.

For a long time, each doctor only focused on their specialty, which made some of Tim's symptoms worse, but I started to track his medi- cations, symptoms, and reactions to each medication. I made sure that each doctor knew what the other doctors were prescribing. In fact, this was more important than it had been before.

We were very fortunate to have so many doctors taking care of Tim, and once they realized that some of his problems were reactions to some of the medications, they would switch him to a different one. I had become a part of the team. It was my job to keep each doctor aware of what was happening. Not only did this help the doctors, but it also helped Tim to realize that I wasn't trying to control or hurt him, as he'd accused me in earlier days, but that I was trying to help. This was a pivotal point in our relationship. I was now his advocate to make sure everyone was on the same page.

It took a while for the doctors to understand. So many of them felt Tim needed to be in a long-term care facility, especially when the emotional outbursts got severe, but once they saw how I handled each situation, I could see and feel the respect that these doctors had for me.

CHAPTER 17

Christmas time always meant excitement in our household. I would start the inside decorating right after Halloween, putting up two to three Christmas trees inside. Garlands hung from the stairway, and big red bows were everywhere—every inch of the house was decorated. Christmas day was my birthday. My gift to myself was to decorate inside and out, with elegantly themed Christmas trees. On average, twenty to thirty thousand lights would decorate the outside. This was so important to me as I would sit by the window or out on the porch, watching and hearing the cheers and seeing the happiness as people passed by. Sharing this holiday magic was something I looked forward to every year.

Tim had told me the first Christmas we were together that I overdid it, but after that first night of sitting with me and watching the faces of not only our children but those of families in the neighborhood, he promised never to tell me that again.

But this year was a little different. My health hadn't been very good for a few months. Between my MS and infections that I kept getting, I was quite a bit weaker and knew that I would have to take it easy. I had the inside perfect and part of the outside complete when I started to feel an unbearable pain in my left foot. I had twisted my ankle laying lights out on the hill off the lake, and my ankle was so swollen, I knew it needed to be x-rayed.

Within a few hours, I was told that I had torn my Achilles tendon and my plantar fascia, and my heel bone had a crack in it. I would need to have surgery as soon as possible. I was so upset—who was going to finish the Christmas lights, and what would happen with all the progress I had made with Tim, with keeping our schedule? The only thing I kept thinking was at least it was my left foot—I would still be able to drive, but I was just mad at myself for getting hurt.

As the doctors were telling me all that would have to be done, and that I wouldn't be able to put any weight on it until weeks after surgery, Tim was sitting there. His response was to say, "No problem, I can drive her wherever she needs to go, and I can take care of everything."

I sat there looking at him in astonishment and said, "It's my left foot so I should be able to drive, but I would love the help." I didn't know if I was going to cry or laugh, but I knew I was in for a lot more struggles: Tim was feeling "better" and thought that he could do this.

After surgery, I came home in the afternoon with three screws and so many stitches but no cast. My foot was continuing to swell, and the surgeon didn't want me to have any complications.

Tim was a champ that first night I was home. I had made some meals up before the surgery and set everything up so he would feel like he could do this, and it worked out well. Tim was happy with himself and had found a little confidence that he had been missing for a long time.

Tim's newfound confidence was a good thing at times, though sometimes it was hard for me to keep him from wanting to "drive" and "do things" that he should not be doing. I had never had his licenses revoked, even though the doctors had recommended it years earlier. I simply always drove, and he was okay with that and didn't feel I was taking something away from him. The kids never asked why I drove all the time, and I just let it go.

One afternoon, he was determined to drive, to go get something from the store, and I was panicked. I was stuck on the couch as he walked out the door with the keys. I tried to stop him, but he was gone faster than I could get to him. As I sat on the edge of the couch, my heart was pounding. Tim hadn't really driven by himself in almost two years. I was overcome with emotion. I just sat there crying and wondering: Would he get lost? Would he return? Where was he going?

About thirty minutes later, Tim walked in through the door. He could see that I had been crying and asked, "Did you hurt yourself?"

I said, "No, I was worried about you."

He let out a little giggle like a young boy who'd gotten caught doing something wrong. Then he started to rub the brim of his cap, and he said, "I am, too. I am not comfortable driving alone." That day, he promised me he would never drive alone again, and he told me he'd prefer to be a passenger only.

Finally weeks later I had healed, and we got back on our daily schedule. Tim had missed quite a few classes at the wellness center, and I could see that his physical health had started to decline. He was losing his balance more frequently, and his strength in his arms and legs was weakening.

The wellness center required us to get a release for Tim to continue with his classes. We would need to go to his doctor to get the clearance so that he could continue his classes.

We hadn't seen the neurologist for a couple of months. He was surprised to see the decline and voiced his concerns that Tim needed to get back to his classes and start exercising again. The doctor didn't like what he was seeing, and he made a point of telling me that I needed to focus more on Tim, or this could become a problem.

I wasn't sure what the doctor was trying to say. Was he thinking I was being neglectful, or was Tim in such a decline that the doctor didn't know if he could come back?

So I asked him, and he answered simply, "Sometimes we have to know when we need help."

I said in reply, "I am not there yet. We're fine."

The doctor was focusing on Tim's needs. I understood this, but I knew we could get back to where we'd been before I had my surgery.

The guilt was overwhelming. The doctor handed me a brochure about the stages of Parkinson's, and as we left the office, I wondered if I was wrong. Was it possible that I was not capable of taking care of Tim anymore?

I decided to put that thought in the back of my mind and to get focused, I wasn't going to let Tim go downhill because I had been hurt.

We left the office with the doctor's okay for Tim to continue his classes. I drove straight to the wellness center. Tim participated in a late exercise class, and even though he was weaker, I could see how happy he was to be back in class. He worked hard and even took time to tell everyone about how much he'd "helped" me while I was down with my foot.

While Tim was in his class, I looked over the brochure the doctor had handed me. Now the thoughts were running through my mind: What if I didn't ask the right questions? Was I losing my focus?

The brochure was informative, but I had heard most of this at the wellness center over the last few months. It covered managing Parkinson's disease in the later stages and addressed the caregiver or care partner of someone with Parkinson's disease in the late stages.

I read through the list of all the symptoms. The brochure went on to say that the role of the caregiver could vary based on the needs of their loved one. I sat there thinking. Was the doctor trying to tell me that Tim had moved into the later stages?

It hit me: I needed to pay attention to the symptoms. I was now more frightened than I had been in a long time.

CHAPTER 18

I became almost obsessed with making sure Tim's health would come first. I drove him to class Monday through Friday and made sure we made it to the support group meetings.

Tim seemed to be doing better. His attitude was more positive than it had been in a long time, which helped at home. He was focused on his health and wanting to be there for the children. When they would come to visit, having them around was a positive point in our lives for both Tim and me.

We made it through a couple of months without any major problems. The doctors were happy to see the improvements in Tim. I loved to watch Tim at his appointments; he was like a child who was so proud of himself for getting an A on a class project. He was proud of himself and happy with the success he was having with all of his classes.

The more Tim worked out, the worse his breathing became. He was on numerous inhalers. The pulmonologist couldn't figure out why he was wheezing and struggling to catch his breath. He was almost certain it was the Parkinson's, but the neurologist didn't believe that this was the case. In the end, we really didn't get answers, we just kept doing the exercises that both doctors recommended.

Within a week, I had to rush Tim to the hospital. He was struggling to breathe, and his lips were blue, scaring us both. They ran every test and found that he had atelectasis, a fairly common condition that happens when tiny sacs in your lungs, called alveoli, don't inflate but collapse, making it difficult to breathe. They diagnosed Tim with COPD, chronic obstructive pulmonary disease, a progressive disease that makes it hard to breathe. "Progressive" means the disease gets worse over time. It was one more thing for us to worry about.

Tim spent a couple of days in the hospital. Since he'd never been a smoker, they were trying to figure out why he had developed this. Also, with all the other health problems, they wanted to make sure he was stable enough to go home. We now had another problem that had no cure. The goals of the treatment were to relieve the symptoms, slow the progression of the disease, and continue to exercise. They told us that the more active you are, the better it is for the lungs.

Over the next few weeks, Tim was anxious, and his paranoia seemed to increase in response to one of the inhalers he had to use. There wasn't really a choice for a different medication, so this would be something I would just have to deal with and make sure the family understood this. At that time, the visits from friends and family started to decrease again, but we still had the wellness center, and the friendships we had there were strong.

Over time, no matter where we went, Tim would sit down and lean back. I always asked him if he was okay, and his response was no longer "awesome" but "I'm okay." Between the Parkinson's, dementia, and the COPD, he was exhausted, but he never admitted to it. Everyone would ask what was going on, and I sometimes felt embarrassed when he'd say nothing even though he was sitting or lying like a doll made out of cloth.

I knew Tim wasn't well, but when we would go into a doctor's office, he acted like he was fantastic. When I would try to explain what was happening, he would get so upset that he would even tell the doctor maybe he should have gotten that divorce the first doctor had recommended to him. Even though his memory was failing, that story was still his go-to story when he felt frustrated by the things I was doing or saying.

I had stopped taking things as personally as I had at first. I kept telling myself that it wasn't Tim that was acting this way, it was the diseases that were making him like this. I even said this to myself every morning before getting out of bed, like a morning mantra. While it helped, there were still times when my health made me act in a way that made me feel guilty. I always knew that a lot of caregivers have this guilt and that a caregiver has to try to let go of this kind of guilt. For myself, it was hard, but I tried. I now was experiencing what so many others had, and finally understood how hard it was to let go of the guilt.

CHAPTER 19

We were coming out of a really brutal summer. The heat had been unbearable, and I was waiting for Halloween night, as this usually meant cooler nights and the beginning of the holiday season. While we were still experiencing temperatures that were ten degrees above normal, temperatures in the upper seventies and eighties were better than the more than 115 days we'd had above 100 and the fifteen nights that never dropped below ninety. We had both been miserable.

I decided that with Tim's health being so poor and our youngest heading to college in a few months, I was going to make this the best holiday season we'd ever had. With four adult children, one almost there, and two grandchildren, we were blessed, and I wanted this season to be some of our finest memories for all of us!

Starting with Halloween, I planned a huge party out in front of our home and invited all the neighbors to join our family. Everyone wore costumes. I made chili and other treats to feed everyone. We laughed and enjoyed ourselves that night, and I was elated that my plan seemed to be working.

My next step was going to be Thanksgiving. I had hosted the entire family for years. It was always a special day; I had always made sure all the Christmas lights would light for the first time Thanksgiving night. This year, though, was even more special: Tim would be turning fifty-five—or "double nickels" as he would call it. Since everyone would be at the house, I planned the decorations to include pictures of Tim and memories of past birthdays.

Tim was overwhelmed but happy. I was worried as I could see he was struggling to breathe, but I didn't want to ruin his day. I would just let him tell me if he needed help.

We made it through the Thanksgiving birthday party, and I loved seeing the joy in my family's faces. Their hugs for me and Tim at the end of the night were heartfelt and authentic. It had been a while since I'd felt this way. Tim was so happy that it brought tears to his eyes as he thanked me for loving him and making his day one that he would never forget.

We always went shopping Thanksgiving night for Black Friday. This time, some of the kids met up with us. Even though we really weren't buying anything, we were amazed at how much fun we had. When we finally got home, I remember that I silently cried myself to sleep. I hadn't been this happy in a long time, and I didn't want it to stop.

Five days later, Tim was sick again, and this time I made him go to the hospital. He was getting more stubborn as the days went by, and he fought me all the way.

I was scared. He was choking and turning blue. He kept complaining of chest pains. I knew that this could be the COPD, but I wanted to make sure it wasn't his heart; that seemed to be the only thing left that was healthy.

This time, he was in the hospital for six days, and he wasn't able to attend the wellness classes for almost two weeks. I knew that we would have to get back on our schedule soon. Now he was lying down all the time, and he had a new saying: "My recliner is calling me."

When Tim was released from the hospital, he just sat and stared at the Christmas trees. He had started feeling both his mom's and dad's spirits around the house.

I did, too. It was like the whole family was around us all the time. This meant a lot to Tim.

Christmas morning at five a.m., all our children and grandchildren came to our house. Santa Claus had been very good to the family, and each person had a stocking and over fifteen gifts to open. I loved doing this, and I kept thinking that it would give us something to look forward to every year and that maybe the kids would want to be with us on Christmas morning.

CHAPTER 20

We rang in the New Year 2014 with family, food, and fire-works, making all my hopes for a wonderful holiday season complete. All our children and extended family had the best time, and they continued to thank us every time we saw them. I was already looking forward to next year.

Over the next several weeks, Tim had to be admitted to the hospital three more times. The breathing problems that had started so many months earlier continued with no relief, and his lungs were weakening every day. The atelectasis continued to worsen. His lungs weren't working well. At times, he would need oxygen, but the doctors assured us that everything was fine, deep breathing would help, and Tim needed to get back to his exercises.

I was frustrated, I felt like we were just being told this because there was nothing that could help and they were just trying to keep us positive. It was the same kind of thing we had been told every time he was diagnosed with something new: *Stay positive and keep active.*

But I couldn't stop wondering why his lungs were getting worse. Was this because of his Parkinson's, or was this part of the dementia? Was he not breathing correctly? My questions continued, but there never seemed to be an answer or reason.

When Tim was being discharged from the hospital, I asked if they would be sending him home with oxygen. The doctor felt that if Tim needed oxygen, he should be in the hospital, and so he refused to prescribe it for him.

In contrast, I knew that Tim did so much better on the oxygen, and I just couldn't understand why the doctors felt this way. When I questioned them, they said that oxygen could make him worse if he used too much.

By this time, I was angry. They kept admitting him to the hospital. I knew that I could control his use of oxygen, but it seemed that the doctors had started to lose faith in me, they did not know why Tim had to be admitted to the hospital so many times.

As soon as we got home, I started to look for an oxygen condenser. I found one that only had a few hours on it, so I bought it and set it up at home. Using it, Tim rested more easily, and he didn't need to use his inhalers as frequently.

I told the neurologist what I had done, and he responded with the first smile I'd seen from him in months. He said he didn't understand why the other doctors didn't want Tim to have oxygen at home. He thanked me for being honest.

I was finally doing something right, at least in this doctor's eyes.

Out of the many times and different situations when I advocated for Tim, sometimes I was ignored, but this time, I did what I knew was right. Doing the right thing can be hard because you think about how much time and money these people spend to become doctors, and they aren't worried about the patient. However, sometimes it can be about how much money is going into their pockets. Tim should have been prescribed oxygen months earlier, something that was proven at his next pulmonologist's visit, when all his breathing tests and blood work showed improvement.

By Valentine's day, Tim had started to feel a little better. At this point, he was able to attend his wellness classes one or two times a week. I knew it wasn't enough, but he was so exhausted, he just couldn't make it more than that. He began to eat more as if he was starving all the time. This worried me. He was putting on weight, and

I was already struggling to help him with getting dressed. If he were to fall, he was too heavy for me to even try to help him up.

Tim had an appointment in March with his neurologist. We hadn't seen this doctor in a few weeks. He noticed the weight change and asked Tim if he was having troubles with food.

Tim rubbed his belly and said, "No, the food likes me just fine."

I smiled a little, but the doctor looked at me sharply as he had done in previous visits. He told me I needed to get Tim's weight down as this wasn't good for his breathing or his balance. The doctor was pleased with Tim's oxygen levels, however, and repeated his advice that we should use it as we needed to.

I wonder sometimes if he had a clue about the extent of Tim's behavior. I had always thought it was normal for a Parkinson's patient to be a little challenging; this was what I had seen in so many of the others at the wellness center. Here this doctor was, trying to get me to make Tim stop eating, which would be a chore, maybe even impossible.

Even though I knew Tim wouldn't be happy, I quit baking cookies and cakes. I cut out all desserts and sodas for Tim and reminded him many times every day that the doctor wanted him to lose twenty pounds before his next visit in six weeks.

Tim was never compliant. He would get up in the middle of the night, and I would catch him making himself a bowl of cereal or eating crackers. In fact, he was starting to remind me of his father more and more every day, I would find candy hidden in the pockets of his recliner, and I never knew where it would come from.

Tim had been trying to stay busy. Our youngest was raising her last pig for FFA, and he tried so hard to participate. He would have me take him to the school.

He was excited about the upcoming auction. Our daughter had always done well in the auctions. Her pigs were as important to her as they were to us. This was one last family thing that we were doing before she left home for college.

Tim was struggling emotionally. He didn't know what his life would look like without her at home. Many nights, he cried about it. His emotions were high and sometimes uncontrollable.

The only thing I could do was hug him and tell him that we would visit her just like we had with the others. He knew, though, that we hadn't done that much traveling. If he rode in the van for very long, his legs would lock up on him. He didn't want anyone, especially our children, to see him that way.

When I woke one morning around four a.m., I could hear Tim breathing hard. He hadn't needed oxygen for a couple of days, so I woke him and put him on the oxygen. Then, he started to cough, and his chest started to hurt.

I remembered what the pulmonologist had said—that the oxygen could hurt him if it wasn't used at the right time—so I pulled it off and grabbed the oximeter and took his oxygen levels. They were low, meaning he needed it, so I put it back on.

Meanwhile, Tim was starting to panic. He wanted to go to the hospital. This was the first time he'd admitted that he needed to go. But then, when I told him I was going to call an ambulance, he refused.

As I got Tim in the van, his breathing was shallow, and he could barely talk. I was now angry that he wouldn't let me call an ambulance. I drove so fast, we made it to the hospital in less than five minutes. It probably would have taken the ambulance longer to get to the house.

As we walked into emergency, I grabbed a wheelchair standing by the entrance. Tim collapsed as I was sitting him down. The girl at the front desk called a code blue. I have never seen so many people move so fast in my life.

As they wheeled Tim back to the emergency room, he came to and said, "Hey slow down, my wife is old." All of sudden, he was fine, he wasn't struggling to breathe anymore. If the personnel hadn't seen how blue he was, they would never have believed me.

They started to run tests, and within a few hours, they admitted him for observation. They hadn't found anything, but they were concerned enough to keep him overnight. Within a couple hours, he had another attack, but the same thing happened: he came out of it as if nothing were wrong.

After all that had happened, I wondered if using the oxygen might have been the problem so I told the doctors what I had done. That was the first time they admitted that they'd made a mistake not prescribing a unit for him. I had probably saved his life by having it there when he needed it.

This made me feel better, but now I was concerned about what else they weren't telling me. Everyone in the hospital knew I had Tim's power of attorney and made all the medical decisions. They knew he had dementia and couldn't make these decisions himself.

I just kept feeling like I wasn't being told something.

I stayed at the hospital without leaving for two days. The third night, the nurses told me he would be in there for a couple of more days. They said that I should go home and rest for the night, and they would call me if anything came up. I reluctantly left; I needed a shower, and I needed my medication. The stress had brought on a flare with my MS, and I knew if I didn't get my medicine, I might end up in a bed in the same hospital.

The next day, I went to the hospital. As I entered the room, startling him when I opened the door, Tim was trying to get dressed.

"What are you doing?" I asked him. I thought maybe he was confused and didn't know what he was doing.

He answered, "I'm going home. I am done."

I was starting to tell him that he couldn't leave without the doctor's permission when the nurse walked in and said to me, "You got here fast!"

I didn't know what she was talking about. She continued, saying, "It will be a couple of hours before he can leave."

I was confused—the night before, I'd been told he was going to be there at least a couple more days. Now, as I started to question the nurse, an older woman walked in and introduced herself. She was the hospital social worker, and she needed to talk to Tim about some of his options.

Totally confused, I asked her what she was talking about. She said that there wasn't a lot they could do for Tim. He'd told them he wanted to go home, so they were releasing him. I stopped her and asked why I hadn't been notified, reminding her that as his medical power of attorney, the hospital should have notified me.

She glanced over at Tim and said, "Mr. Bird, is it all right to talk in front of your wife?"

He answered, "She's the boss."

I tried to stay calm even though something had happened overnight. The social worker told me that Tim had decided he didn't want to stay, and they couldn't force him. She then said that neither could I, that my power of attorney was only good if he couldn't make verbal decisions. Legally, I had never gone to court to have him deemed unable to make his own decisions.

This was the first time anyone had ever said that to me in over six years. At every hospital and doctor visit, I had made all the decisions. They all knew that Tim's dementia kept him from making these kinds of decisions, but this social worker was going by the book, and Tim was going home.

Tim was happy. As he started to walk out the door, the social worker asked him where he was going, and Tim answered with fire in his eyes, "Home! You said I don't have to listen to anyone, and that includes you."

I could tell by the look on the social worker's face that she was confused. She reached for his arm to try to stop him, but Tim looked at her and said, "You are treating my wife terrible, and I am not going to put up with this. I need her to help me. You don't know what you are talking about."

I quickly got in front of Tim and told him she was only doing her job, that only we knew what was going on in our life, and nothing was changing. I would still be there to help him.

As Tim started to calm down, I added, "Look, you are still in your hospital gown. We have to get you dressed."

His eyes softened as he looked down and saw that he wasn't dressed.

I asked the social worker if she could step out while we got Tim dressed. I could see the frustration in her eyes. The nurse who had been helping us asked the social worker if she could talk to her. They stepped out of the room, and the door closed behind them.

At that moment, Tim started to cry. "Why are they trying to take you away from me?"

I hugged him and told him that it would be over my dead body. I tried to explain to him that the social worker didn't know us. I kept repeating it, thinking in the back of my mind that I should never have gone home the night before. Something had happened, and Tim couldn't communicate it to me.

As I finished helping Tim get dressed, I could hear the nurse talking to the social worker in the hallway, though not loud enough that I could understand what she was saying. Then I heard a light knock at the door. Before I could answer, the door opened. It was the nurse, wanting to know if we needed help.

Tim smiled and said, "I can't find my baseball cap."

It took me a minute to remember that he hadn't had it on when we'd left the house in such a rush. When I told him that I'd forgotten it and it was at home, he looked at me and said, "I forgive you."

The social worker was waiting to finish our conversation. I told Tim I was going to invite her back into the room and that she would be nice. I went to the door, and when I opened it, she was standing right there, just staring at me.

I asked her to come in, that we were ready to hear about Tim's discharge plans. The nurse that had been so helpful started to leave the room, but Tim asked her to stay and said that he didn't like the other lady. Even though discharge was a busy time for the nurses, she agreed.

As the social worker turned to Tim, I could see that whatever the nurse had told her had changed her approach. She kept eye contact with Tim and slowly began to speak. "Mr. Bird, I'm sorry. I would never want you to think that I wasn't going to let your wife help you with your decisions, but you're the one who told me earlier this morning that you weren't going to do any more tests or treatments. I just made my discharge plan to include your wishes."

I was taken aback by this. Because I hadn't known that any decision had been made earlier in the morning, I asked her about those decisions. She answered me almost as if I were a child. "Mr. Bird doesn't want to stay. He doesn't want any more treatments, he just wants to go home."

As I tried to get more information, no one was saying anything, so I asked Tim, "What is going on? Why won't you talk to me?" Tears came to my eyes, and the only thing I could think of was when Jim had decided he didn't want help anymore, and there was nothing any of us could do. Now it seemed as if Tim was doing the same thing.

Suddenly, Tim looked at me and said, "I just hate this place. I come here, and they do nothing."

I looked at the social worker and asked her what this meant.

She opened the folder in her hand and handed me a brochure for a palliative care service.

I started to panic. "You want to put him on hospice?"

She said, "No, this service can do treatments from home. Mr. Bird can still see all of his doctors, and they can even handle some of the problems that you've come to the emergency room with."

I had heard about this but didn't have any knowledge of how the program worked. This was new since I'd been in the industry. I started to look through the brochure. My interest had been piqued as I knew that if they could take care of Tim at home when we had problems, it would make our lives a lot easier, and Tim would be more at ease.

I asked if we had to go to a social worker to find out more, and she answered, "They are on their way to talk to you now."

I looked over at the nurse, still waiting patiently, and told her she could go if she wanted, that we would know more after we talked to the palliative care people. As the nurse headed to the door, another knock sounded.

Tim was getting frustrated. "I want to go home!"

I gently took his arm and told him that it wouldn't be long. The door opened to admit two more women, one in her sixties and the other in her late twenties.

Tim looked right at the younger woman and asked, "You coming home with me?"

She smiled and said, "If you would like. We have a great program that will help keep you out of the hospital."

Tim answered, "Where do I sign? It's already Thursday, and baseball is on."

I chuckled inside, thinking that this would be an easy transition for us. Tim didn't want to be in the hospital, and they could help keep him out.

As Tim flirted with the younger woman, it gave me time to read more about the program, where I learned they were a hospice and palliative care company. I looked up and asked how they decided which program that applied, and she said, "Whatever the doctor feels is appropriate. With hospice, you have to have qualifying conditions—yes, Tim has them, but his doctor has recommended palliative care."

I was relieved. Even though I knew that hospice isn't a death sentence, our children wouldn't see it that way. The only experience they've had was with their grandfather, and he'd passed quickly.

Tim signed the papers. As he didn't have a clue what was going on, they had him sign a paper stating that I was to make all decisions, that he wasn't capable of making them for himself. I was almost uncomfortable with this; even though I'd been making decisions for him, I'd always talked to him, and we would agree together. Now it seemed like he just didn't care anymore.

CHAPTER 21

As we drove home from the hospital, my phone was ringing, and text messages were coming in. I had sent a text to all of the children that their dad was okay and being released from the hospital and that we would like to see everyone at the house on Saturday morning. Every single one of them wanted to know why, so I sent a group message to them that we wanted to talk to them all at the same time.

When we got home, the palliative care workers were waiting for us. I wondered what they were going to do. We had already signed all the paperwork. It turned out that they were just there to introduce themselves and leave some supplies, gloves, masks, and different items that might be needed to take care of Tim at home. I remembered this from when Jim was put on hospice. They paid for everything, but they wanted to make sure the supplies would be there if needed.

Saturday came, and the kids all got to the house early. Their concern was plain on their faces. I hugged each of them as they came in. The only one not there was our second to the youngest; she was in her last semester at NAU, and it was too far for her to travel, but she agreed to be a part of the conversation by speakerphone.

Tim was in his recliner. He didn't get up to hug the kids; they all reached out to him and kissed him on the top of his head. His body was trembling, and the kids thought it was his Parkinson's, but I knew it was nervousness.

I started the conversation after I encouraged everyone to sit down, trying to explain the whole situation and what had happened when I'd gone back to the hospital the morning of Tim's discharge. Watching each of them, I could see the tears in their eyes.

The oldest one spoke up, sounding almost angry. "Why are we just being told about this? If my father is dying, we should know."

I could hear sniffles coming from the speakerphone, so I stood up and walked over to Tim. I asked him, "Tim, are you dying?"

He got a smile and said, "One day."

I said, "No. Have you been told you're dying?"

He grabbed my hand and said, "No, I am fine. I just don't want to go to the hospital. They never find anything wrong with me!"

I could see relief in the faces of the children in the room with us, but I could hear sobbing over the speakerphone. I asked everyone to please be quiet. "Nik, are you okay?"

She answered that she would be. She was just relieved that he was okay.

I saw some smiles across the room and knew that once again, these wonderful children had pulled it together.

We started talking about what was going to happen over the next few weeks. Nik was concerned about her father traveling to a higher altitude for her graduation, that he might need oxygen.

Then the youngest said, "Do you think you guys will make it to my graduation?" She was finishing up her senior year, in high school. We both assured her we would be there, and she told us not to forget that it was outside and they were predicting temperatures above 100 degrees. Not only was she worried about her dad, but she had watched me struggle with my MS in the heat for fourteen years.

We reassured everyone that everything was still going to happen as planned, and as long as their dad was feeling up to it, we would be there. In the back of my mind, I wondered, and I caught myself forcing a smile. I didn't want them to think or feel I was trying to hide something. Honestly, I still didn't know what had happened at the hospital to put this palliative care plan in motion.

I had made breakfast and told everyone to help themselves. While they ate, I picked up my phone to talk to Nik for a while. She was sounding better, though she was very stressed about her finals. I tried to let her know that I was proud of her and that we would keep in contact. I let her know that we had already made our reservations for the hotel and we would be seeing her soon.

She said, "I love you, Momma." That was the first time I had heard that from her in a while. She would never know what a comfort it was for me.

I wanted to keep talking, but we were interrupted when the house phone rang, which was unusual. I looked at the caller ID and saw that the office of Tim's pulmonologist was calling, so I told her that I loved her too, and we hung up.

I answered the home phone, thinking, *This is weird—it's Saturday.* It was the doctor who had visited Tim in the hospital, not the one that we would see in the office. She introduced herself and asked why Tim wasn't in the hospital. I proceeded to tell her what had transpired.

Upset, she said, "You need to take him back now!"

I decided to take the phone outside. I didn't want anyone to see or hear what was going on until I knew more. She started by telling me that Tim's lungs were weak and he need to be on a respirator for at least eight hours a day until they had a chance to heal. I explained to her that no one had told me anything, and Tim had agreed to palliative care.

She said, "He isn't dying, but he needs to give his lungs a chance to rest."

I was confused and started to ask questions. Why did they let him go? What happened?

She had no clue, and I didn't know how I would be able to get Tim back to the hospital. I knew he wasn't going to go without a fight.

I told her I would call her back as soon as I'd talked to Tim, but I didn't think I could change his mind. I kept thinking about the paper he'd signed, giving me total control, and wondering if I should use it and make him go. As soon as I'd hung up, I put a call out to the palliative care people. They had told us they could do any treatment at home, so I wanted some answers before I talked to Tim.

I went back into the house, and at the look on my face, Tim and two of the kids asked in unison, "What's wrong?"

I said, "I got a call from one of your dad's doctors, and I need to take him outside and talk to him." There was no way I could hide this one.

Tim got up from his recliner and followed me out. The youngest one tried to follow, but I asked her to let me talk to her dad alone.

I started to tell Tim about the telephone call I'd just had, and he said, "I know, but they told me my lungs would take care of themselves. That's why I came home."

I now knew that this had happened when I wasn't at the hospital. I could only imagine how upset Tim had been when they'd tried to convince him he needed to do this. That was why the social worker had kept saying that Tim had the right to decide what he wanted to do.

I told Tim we were calling the doctor back right now, and I picked up my cell phone and went to call her back, but the number was on the phone in the house. I had him wait while I went in to get the other phone.

The kids were all looking at the door when I walked in. I spoke before any of them could say anything. "We have to call a doctor back—it's important. I'll explain it when we're done."

I walked back outside, and we called the doctor. Tim told her that he wasn't going back to the hospital and he was feeling fine. I explained that palliative care was looking into what we could do at home.

The doctor answered me sharply. "They aren't going to bring a $100,000 piece of equipment to you!"

I asked her, if he didn't go to the hospital, would he die?

She said, "No, but he won't get better, which could lead to his death, sooner than later."

Now wondering if I should make him go, I asked her how long he would have to be on the machine, and she said, "Probably a few weeks."

Knowing that Tim wasn't in immediate danger, I told her we would wait to hear back from palliative care.

We went back into the house, and I explained to the children about what the doctor had said.

Tim interrupted. "I am not going to the hospital, and that's it."

The fear returned to their faces, but I pulled out the oximeter and showed them how even without oxygen, he was in the low 90s, which was still safe. Then I put the oxygen on him, and it went to 99%, making everyone—including myself—feel better.

Within an hour, the palliative care team called and told us exactly what the doctor had said. They wouldn't place this respirator in our home; if we wanted to do this, Tim would have to go to the hospital. They also stated that once he started, he couldn't just stop—he would have to stay in the hospital and complete the treatment, and it could possibly be months. With all of our plans and all the promises we'd made, Tim wouldn't agree, and this wasn't something I was willing to make him do.

CHAPTER 22

As I was going through some major decisions that needed to be made, I noticed that Tim didn't want to move from his recliner too much. Although once in a while, we would go see the pigs, he had stopped all his classes at the wellness center, and he just wanted to rest and watch television. I found myself serving him his meals in his recliner, and some nights he even slept there. I worried because I could see that when he did move around, he was stiff and sore. He wasn't getting enough exercise to help with the Parkinson's, and it was difficult to get him to understand the problem.

As the days went by, I knew that Tim would need to build up his strength if he was going to be able to attend both of the girls' graduations. He was spending so much time in his recliner, I was trying to figure out a way to put wheels on it so I would be able to push him. I knew that he needed to move, but the constant pushback was wearing me down.

We continued to see all of Tim's doctors in their offices, and the palliative care group would send a doctor once a week and a nursing aide every other day. This helped us both to stay focused on our care plan, but my main concern was how I was going to get Tim to the graduations, and how we'd take his oxygen with us, the machine was heavy and very large, and he would need it, especially in northern Arizona, where the altitude is over seven thousand feet.

One afternoon, we went to the pulmonologist to see if they could help us to get a prescription for a portable machine, but the doctor didn't want Tim to travel so he refused to write the prescription. Knowing that there was no way I was going to break our promise to the girls, I would have to find a way. Then I remembered that the palliative care group had told us they could get us whatever we needed.

I was almost proud of myself for remembering the palliative care group, but the feeling didn't last long. They explained that Tim was still under the care of his doctors, and if they weren't recommending him to travel, the team couldn't go against those wishes. They had to follow the guidelines of the primary care doctors for each diagnosis that Tim had. Even if the neurologist approved it, they still couldn't do it; all the doctors had to agree.

I collapsed into a chair and started to sob. I was struggling with Tim, and the only thing he was looking forward to was an upcoming visit from his brother, the one that also had Parkinson's, and then the girls' graduations.

I had promised. I felt defeated, and my body ached for emotional relief. Crying was the only thing that didn't take any effort, the tears just flowed.

As the doctor from the palliative care group watched me struggle, she handed me a tissue and said, "There is something else we can do." I was ready to hear anything. I was trying to make this happen, so I asked her what she was thinking.

"Tim qualifies for hospice care—he has since the day he was put on palliative care, but none of the doctors would recommend it. But now that I am the doctor on record, I could recommend it, and we could get you everything you need."

As she spoke, I could feel the pressure from crying starting to release, and I asked her, "So what does that mean?"

She took a deep breath and said, "We move him to hospice, get him everything he needs to be comfortable, and make sure he gets to take this trip."

A few weeks earlier, I had told them we weren't ready to move Tim to hospice, but now, here I was, thinking about it so we could go out and enjoy ourselves when his brother came to town, and we could make both graduations.

But what about Tim? Was he ready to do this?

The doctor could see I was panicking, and she finished by saying, "We can always move him back to palliative care if you aren't happy with just one doctor—that would be me—and our hospice service."

My head was spinning—two main thoughts kept swirling around. No more doctors' office visits, for one thing. The second was that this would help fulfill all of Tim's wishes about seeing his daughters graduate. Most of all, not being stuck in the house would be a good place to start, and having portable oxygen would be a blessing.

Tim's cognitive awareness had gone downhill, but no one had ever said anything to indicate Tim could be dying. While the thought had crossed my mind, with so many medical problems going on, at that moment, I wasn't thinking about it. I just wanted to make sure we made it to the girls' graduations. As I was staring blankly into space, the hospice doctor asked me if I wanted her to talk to Tim about it.

All of a sudden, I heard a loud "NO!" Tim was standing in the doorway, and I was shocked by his answer. I looked over to him, and he said, "No one has to talk to me. If I can get oxygen and go out, I want it."

I was pleased but not sure that he was understanding the whole situation. He'd have to go on hospice care, and he would no longer be able to see all his doctors.

The doctor looked at Tim and said, "That's a good thing. You need to have a better quality of life, and you shouldn't be stuck in the house."

I pushed back and had to explain about his doctors and everything that going on to hospice meant, not only to him but to the family.

I reminded him of how the family had reacted when his father had gone on hospice and we had known Jim wasn't wanting to fight for his life.

Tim said, "A smart person once told my dad, 'You can always come off hospice.'"

He was throwing my own words right back at me. I had said this to his father two years earlier. In moments like these, I wondered about his dementia. He remembered a lot—when he wanted to.

Within a few hours, the paperwork was signed, and Tim had his portable oxygen machine. The first thing he wanted to do was to go see the pigs. We were coming up on the last pig show that our daughter would be showing in, and he was excited. His brother and sister-in-law would be flying in, and he finally had so much to look forward to.

CHAPTER 23

C alling the family together for a Sunday dinner had gotten to be almost a weekly event, so none of our kids had any idea of what we were going to be telling them this Sunday. I was nervous, but Tim was doing so much better. Our youngest knew, but she never talked to us about it. She waited until we had our family time to say anything.

As the others came into the house, they could see that Tim was up and about and had his portable oxygen machine. They assumed that his doctors had finally approved it, but then our youngest just blurted out, "No, Dad is on hospice."

The shock in the room, including mine, was apparent. It was the first time all of us were gathered together in a room and no one was talking.

Tim spoke up. "My other doctors wouldn't give me a portable machine. They wanted me to stay down, and I want to be up and doing things."

Our daughter in the medical field said, "Don't you think that's because your lungs are so bad? They need to heal."

That was truly the first time I'd thought about that, but Tim looked at her and said, "This is my choice." I could see the tension now; every-one—including myself—was starting to worry: Would he overdo, and would this make him worse?

Tim addressed us all in a very abrupt voice, and with a look in his eyes I had never seen before, he said, "I know what is good for me.

I am only fifty-five years old. I have a long life to live, and I am not going to do it in a chair."

Our youngest was the first to get up and hug her dad. She said, "I love you, Daddy." All the others followed her lead. This was Tim's decision, and they all knew that they would just have to accept it.

The dinner went well, and everyone was excited at the thought of seeing their aunt and uncle. This would be the first time since he was diagnosed with Parkinson's that Tim's brother would travel to Arizona. He'd had an adaptive brain stimulator surgically implanted a few months earlier, and it had improved some of his Parkinson's symptoms. He was doing well, and it was something we were all excited to see. Maybe, in the future, this could help Tim.

Tim was so improved, not only physically but emotionally. The portable oxygen gave him the freedom and confidence to do the things he wanted to do. When his brother and sister-in-law arrived, they were surprised to see how well he was doing. His brother was almost as excited as we were to go to the pig show at the country fair. He hadn't been to one in years.

Tim and his brother spent some quality time together. It was good for both of them. Even though he and his wife were struggling with the idea of Tim being on hospice, they could see that Tim needed his oxygen to move around. However, they felt he needed all his other doctors to deal with his Parkinson's.

I had noticed that Tim was tiring a lot more easily since they'd arrived. I tried to get him to slow down and rest, but he was tough on me, almost abusive. I tried to talk to him, but he would make remarks to his brother that I was driving him crazy. At night, when we were alone, he kept telling me that he wanted me to back off. I didn't know who this person was, but I hoped he would return to normal after everyone left.

The week went by very quickly. Tim started telling me at night that his mother was visiting him, and she had other spirits with her. I had felt an increase in what I call spiritual activity, but I was so emotionally spent that I couldn't pick up on anything. I was happy that Tim was having these experiences because they were always so comforting for me when I would have them.

The day before his brother and sister-in-law were scheduled to leave, we spent the day at the fairgrounds, watching our daughter show her pig. Tim was happy, but as I watched him, I could see that he was having a tough time trying to breathe. A lot of dust was in the air from the hay and the animals that were being shuffled in out of the arena.

After our daughter showed her pig, Tim looked at me and said, "I have to go." He started coughing, and I could see he was a little blue around the lips. I leaned over and told my sister-in-law that Tim wasn't doing well; they could stay and come home with our daughter, but we had to leave. They left and came with us.

As we were driving home, I looked at Tim. His eyes were closed, and he was holding his chest. The air coming in and out of his lungs was shallow, but the blueness around his lips had started to fade. I glanced in my rearview mirror, and I could see the concern in the faces of his brother and sister-in-law, but no one spoke.

Our youngest called. She was happy about the show. She asked how her dad was doing. I was honest and told her he wasn't well and he needed to rest. She was concerned; she knew when she was around, her dad was always happy and active. She asked if it would be okay if she stayed at her mother's house for the weekend.

I knew that seeing her dad struggle was hard on her, and I was glad that she'd asked. Her mom lived closer to the fairgrounds, and it meant Tim could rest.

The next morning, Tim's brother and sister-in-law were getting ready to head back to Utah. My heart was heavy. I was wanting them to stay. I kept feeling that we might not see them for a while, and even though Tim had been tough on me, he loved being with his brother. They both said goodbye to Tim. Having barely moved from his recliner, he told them he was doing so much better, and he would talk to them soon.

As I walked them out to their car, I hugged them both and told them how scared I was, that we only had a few more weeks until the girls graduated, and I wasn't sure if we would make it. Tim hadn't lasted very long at the fairgrounds. He needed to build his strength back and try to recover.

They both hugged me and said they felt Tim was doing well, that he seemed happy, and they were glad they'd come. As I watched them pull away, I stood there sobbing. Somehow, I knew in my heart that Tim would never see them again.

Later that morning, the hospice doctor had come back to visit and check to see how Tim was doing. I explained about the change in his breathing, and especially the change toward me. His anxiety was worse than it had been, and he seemed more agitated than usual. The doctor had a strange look on his face and said he would send over some medication that could help this.

Tim seemed to be exhausted, and he slept off and on most of the day. I called the kids, and each of them came over at different times. I didn't want Tim to get overwhelmed.

Tim's son is our most emotional one. As he sat with Tim, he started to cry, and his dad assured him he was okay—he just needed to rest. As he spent time with each child, I knew something was going on. After each one would leave, Tim would be angry with me, as if I'd made them leave. When I helped him get up and go to the bathroom, he pushed me away. Even when I came back to help him, he would ask me where I'd gone, as if he didn't know that he'd pushed me away.

The next day was like Grand Central Station for hospice workers. The doctor came back, for which I was grateful, and he stated that he was going to send over the social worker, a nurse, and the aide to help. He could see I was exhausted and needed to rest.

I was relieved to get some help. The aide offered to fix lunch, and I was thinking Tim hadn't eaten in over twenty-four hours, and he really wasn't drinking much. When I offered him water, he would take a sip—but not as much as he should have. The aide told me this was normal and not to worry about it.

I thought to myself, *This isn't normal for Tim.*

When the social worker arrived and the doorbell rang, I was in the hallway with Tim. I said, "Come in!"

Tim started yelling at me. "I'm right here! What do you want?" He wasn't aware that the doorbell had rung.

The social worker came in and asked if I needed any help. I told her I was okay and that we would be done in a minute. Tim had gotten up four or five times to go to the bathroom to urinate, but nothing was coming out, and of course, that was my fault, too!

The social worker sat and watched for a while. Then, as she started to speak, Tim interrupted. "Hey, my mom is here!"

The social worker looked around. She knew that Tim's mom had died years ago, but he was so convincing, she thought he was talking about my mom.

My cell phone rang. I looked at the caller ID. It was our youngest's mother.

That made me nervous. I hadn't heard from our youngest. She was supposed to be at the auction with her pig.

Her mother began to speak, and I could feel my heart start to race as she said, "I know that things aren't good over there, and I don't want my daughter around if her father is dying. I am having her stay here until I know more of what is going on."

I thought to myself, did our youngest think her dad was dying? I told her mother that this hadn't even been talked about, and I wasn't sure if that was what was going on, and I didn't know if that would be best for either one of them.

She answered me, saying, "That's too bad. You will call me first."

I agreed—reluctantly. I wondered why she was trying to be a mother now; she had always trusted me, but now something had changed. I couldn't worry about it right now. Tim had to be my main focus.

I hung up and started to cry. It wasn't the first time she had made me cry, but I had never shown this type of frustration in front of anyone before. Being a step-parent, I had my own personal rule: Never say anything bad about the other parent. The children come first. I wasn't going to break that rule now, especially with their dad being so sick.

The social worker came over and put her arm around me. She said, "We are going to get through this together."

I thought, *What is she talking about? What are we trying to get through?* As I was trying to get my thoughts together, Tim tried to get up to go to the bathroom again. I took him, and again, nothing came out.

As I was walking him back to his recliner, he pushed me so hard, I fell to the ground. The social worker jumped up to help me, and Tim blamed her for making me fall.

I didn't know how much I could handle at this point. I was weak, and my emotions were high.

The social worker went to the refrigerator and got out some drops that the pharmacy had dropped off earlier. As she was giving them to Tim, I thought it was morphine, and I said, "He hasn't complained about any pain."

She told me that this was a medication to calm Tim down, that with this and the morphine, it would help. She was sure that Tim was experiencing pain, and the two medicines would help with the outbursts.

I sat in a daze. I had known about these medications. We had them in pill form, but the pharmacy had sent them over in drops. When I asked why, she answered, "This will be the only way you will be able to give it to him since he isn't drinking."

I was even more frustrated. I was thinking, *I will make him drink more.*

Then she continued, "Terminal agitation can be hard to deal with."

This was the first time anyone had mentioned the words *terminal* or *death* to me. Only a couple of weeks earlier, we had gotten on hospice so we could get Tim his portable oxygen, and now this woman was sitting here, telling me that my husband was dying. Was I the only one that didn't see it? Was I in such denial that I didn't want to believe it?

In that moment, I thought, *Did going to the fair cause his lungs to shut down? Is this my fault for insisting on the portable oxygen tank?* So many questions—and I just sat there, like I was frozen in time.

This couldn't be true. I pushed back at the social worker. "What makes you think he's dying?"

She said, "He isn't eating or drinking, and he isn't processing anything that is going on." She used the example of him pushing me down and blaming her. "He is having spiritual connection."

I thought, *Well, that is nothing new!*

Then, the final thing she said was like someone hit me over the head with a frying pan. "He is having lack of voluntary activity, he can't urinate, and he hasn't had a bowel movement."

I remembered, hearing her say the words, that these were things we'd looked for in the nursing home where I had worked.

My cell phone rang. It was our youngest. She was excited; her pig had sold, and she had made quite a bit of money. She couldn't wait to come home and show her dad.

Remembering the call from her mother, I told her that her mother wanted her there for the night. Because it was Saturday, I knew I could get a hold of her mother, and I would let her handle it the way she wanted. I didn't want this, but her mother had reminded me that when Tim died, I would no longer be her stepmom—she would be our youngest's only mom.

This wasn't something I even wanted to think about. This little girl had been with me since she was four, and now she was almost eighteen.

As I hung up the phone, I looked at the social worker and told her I had to make a call. This would be one of the most important calls that I would make. I called the mother of our two youngest and told her that I'd just been told that Tim was indeed going to pass away, and that I would let her tell the youngest one what she felt was necessary.

She stated she didn't want me calling the other daughter, but I wasn't going to let that happen. She was a married woman, and this was something I wanted to do. Not only did I see her as my child but as a woman that I loved and respected. Not even her mother would take that away from me.

I then picked up the phone and called each child to explain what was going on. I started with the second to the youngest. I told her that I didn't know how long he had, that I was needing more information, but her dad seemed okay right now. I admitted that I was still struggling with this.

She was crying so hard, I couldn't understand her answer. I went on to tell her that she was the first to get the call and to give me a few minutes to call the others, and we would all talk very soon. I said I had to get more information from hospice, that I still wasn't sure but I might take him to the hospital.

The social worker heard me say this, and she stood up and started to pace around the room. I told my daughter that I had to go. I asked her please to wait until she heard back from me and to please not call her youngest sister, that her mother was wanting to take care of that.

I could hear her frustration and wanted to talk more, but I knew I couldn't. The social worker was now tapping a pen on the table, and all I could hear was the clicking noise of that pen. I told our daughter that I loved her, and I promised to call her back very soon.

The minute I hung up, the social worker came over to me. Inside, I wanted to scream at her. Why was she annoying me? I had decisions to make!

She gently touched my shoulder and said, "Holly, you are more than welcome to take Tim to the hospital, but he must come off of hospice care first."

I thought, *Well then, get it done,* but before I could say anything, she continued. "Last week, when I met with Tim, he told me that if this day were to come, you would fight to keep him alive."

I said, "He knows me well."

She continued. "Tim doesn't want this. He made up his mind. I don't think he knew it would be this soon—none of us did—but this was his choice."

The tears were coming down, and I had no control of my thoughts. I said to her, "He has dementia and doesn't know what he wants."

As I was getting more frustrated, Tim jumped up out of his recliner and said, "I gotta go to the train station, Mom is waiting for me."

I grabbed his hand and tried to lead him back to his recliner, but he turned away and started to climb the stairs. I was scared; he was already unstable, and he had pushed me. I didn't want either of us to get hurt.

The social worker helped me to get him down before he got too far up the stairway. Taking both bottles of drops out of the refrigerator, she said, "You might have to do this every couple of hours to keep him calm. He's a pretty big guy, and the drops wear off pretty quickly."

Within a couple of minutes, Tim was calm and happy. I told him about the pigs, and he fell asleep as I was talking to him.

As Tim was sleeping, I told the social worker I had to call the rest of the kids and figure out what I was going to do to get the paperwork done to take him off hospice.

She asked me to sit down and take a deep breath, and as I looked at her, I saw a blue light around her. I knew that I was supposed to listen: my Angels were giving me a message.

"Tim thinks he is going on a train ride. His mother is here to pick him up. The dying process has begun."

As she was explaining this to me, I was thinking, *No! My mom told him that when he got better, we would go on a train ride.* This was on his bucket list; it had nothing to do with him dying.

She continued, "As I said, Tim told me you would fight for him, but he asked me to make sure you followed his wishes. That is why the doctor had me come to visit."

I caught myself shaking my head in disbelief. The doctor hadn't wanted to tell me without the social worker, so that's why he had sent so many people over. He'd known and didn't want me to call 911 without knowing that this was all normal, Tim was dying, these were his wishes, and this woman sitting next to me was going to make sure I understood what was happening.

I started asking questions. There were things I needed to know before I started calling people. *How long?*—that was the very first question.

She looked at me and said, "If any of us knew how long we were going to be here, this job would be a lot easier."

"Are you going to transfer him to an inpatient facility?"

She answered, "We can, but that will be awhile—he isn't that close."

It seemed that every answer brought more questions. I felt like I was a lost little girl, and no one wanted to help.

CHAPTER 24

I felt alone. The one person who had been with me every day wasn't allowed to come over. Even though we had never even talked about Tim dying, she must have talked to her mom about it. As the social worker continued to try to field all my questions, I knew that this was going to be a long battle, and I needed to look to the people with the hospice group as my team instead of the enemy. I asked the social worker if I could get an electric hospital bed. I would put it where I'd had his father's, in the eating area of the kitchen.

She said that the equipment might take a day or two to get there, that it would be on Monday.

Four hours later, at seven o'clock in the evening, I still hadn't eaten, and the social worker had left. I truly was alone. I had made all the calls to the kids. Even though I couldn't answer how long Tim had, I had hope that he would last long enough at least to be there for the girls when they graduated, even though not in person, but he would be able to talk to them and tell them how proud he was.

The night was a long one. The medicine wore off about an hour after giving it to him, and Tim's outbursts and physical strength were getting louder and stronger. I had to call hospice twice that evening, until they agreed that I could give Tim his medication every hour: the morphine, and then an hour later, the lorazepam, and to switch them back and forth as needed.

Tim continued to wander around the house. If I tried to help, he would push me or hit me to get away. One time, he even tried to go out the front door.

I thought, *If he gets out, he will fall into the lake, and then how will I get him out?* I put a chair up against the door, and I think that confused him as he never tried to go back out that door again.

I convinced Tim to come and lie down with me in our room, which I had moved downstairs so there was no reason to go upstairs at all. This was the first time he lay down with me in over four months. I was surprised when he grabbed me. As he was spooning me from behind, he was holding me so tight, but I didn't want to move. He finally fell asleep, and his grip lightened enough that I could fall asleep at last, too.

I woke up when I felt Tim move, and it startled me. Then he pushed me off the bed onto the floor. I hit my head on the door and was a little dazed.

He asked, "Where is my mom? I can't find my mom!"

I looked at the clock and realized I had been asleep for three hours. I'd missed giving him his medicine. Now it was after midnight, and I didn't want to have to bother anyone at hospice so I gave him a dose of both medicines at once. They had told me I could do this if he got really bad.

When Tim saw me grab one of those bottles, he was like a baby bird with his mouth open, just waiting, as if he knew it would help.

As he was taking his medicine, I noticed a glowing light from the other room. I yelled out, "Hello, anyone there?"

Tim said, "Oh, that's my mom. She's back." He sat down in his recliner and drifted off to sleep. I could feel her—I could feel more than I had felt in a while. The Angels were here, and they were going to help us through this.

Sunday was a good day, even though Tim had to have his medicine. Each of the children came to visit, except the one that was out of town. She called and talked to us for almost an hour.

Tim was happy. He even had a few bites of food and drank some water, which gave me something to be happy about: maybe his strength would come back. Tim was really happy when my mom came over. She spent a couple of hours with us and talked to Tim about going on the train. She told him he needed to get better so we could go. I was just glad that Tim was content and happy.

That night, those words that my mom had so lovingly said to Tim—the train ride—became an ordeal that I wasn't ready for. Tim continued to try to go up the stairs. His mother was waiting for him. He pushed me and fought with me. I finally let him go up, and when he didn't see the train, he was upset.

As I stood next to him, he started to blame me that his mother had left and the train had gone without him. His hallucinations were stronger, but the support I was getting from my Angels was also growing stronger. I knew that he must be getting close to passing; the spiritual guidance was stronger than I had ever felt before.

I finally got Tim down the stairs and gave him more medicine, and I laid down on the couch and set my timer for fifty-five minutes. I had no intentions of letting him get any worse than he already was, but I slept through the timer. At four thirty, I woke up, and Tim was headed back up the stairs. I convinced him that his mother was in the kitchen. He followed me, I gave him his medicine, and he seemed to calm down.

I was never so happy as I was on Monday morning. I knew that the hospice aides and nurses would be there soon. I was bruised all over my arms and face from where Tim had pushed or hit me, though I didn't realize this until the nurse asked me about the last time I'd showered.

I thought, *Wow, it's been two long days. I must stink.*

Then she said, "You have dirt on your face." She sat with Tim while I showered, and this was when I saw how beat-up I looked, even though I hadn't felt anything. I didn't look very good.

While I was showering, the aide called the social worker and the doctor. They were all in the living room by the time I was done showering.

I thought, *Wow, I must have been in there longer than I thought.*

The doctor asked me to sit down. He wanted to know why I was so bruised up. I told him I had taken an aspirin, and I bruise more easily than most people. He wasn't buying it. He knew things were getting bad, but I wasn't sharing it. I didn't want them taking Tim to an inpatient facility. He needed his family, and this could be weeks.

The doctor upped the dose and frequency for the medications and assured me that this would help. Inside, I was relieved but also a little scared. Even though I knew that Tim would have to swallow both bottles of drops completely before it could hurt him, I still worried about how much medicine I was giving him. They reassured me that everyone who has their family on hospice worries about that, but as long as I followed the medication protocol, Tim would be fine.

As it was Monday, I couldn't wait for the hospital bed to get there. I thought for sure this would help Tim stay down and he would be more comfortable, so I reminded them to please get it there as soon as they could. The social worker called the equipment warehouse, and they promised it would arrive that day.

The nurse and the aide helped get Tim all cleaned up, and he was in good spirits. I took the social worker outside to tell her about our night. I hadn't slept. I asked her how could I get through this.

She said, "This could go on for weeks, especially since he's eating."

I knew that others had done this. I was strong enough. I could make it.

She again reminded me that if I needed a break, they could take Tim over for respite care for a few days so I could rest.

I told her I was okay.

The day went smoothly. Even though Tim had some anxious moments, the kids came to visit again, and of course, my mom. I told her she couldn't bring up the train, but Tim brought it up to her. I thought, *Oh no, here we go again,* but she reached for his hand and patted it and told him that she would let him know when it was time for us all to go on the trip, and he had to wait for her to be ready.

This seemed to calm him down as if he understood.

CHAPTER 25

A s the day turned into evening, the bed still hadn't been delivered. I put a call in to hospice, and they said it was on a truck and would be delivered and set up tonight. I was comforted by the thought while in the back of mind I was hoping it was true.

It seemed that every night, after the sun would set, Tim got worse. I knew it wasn't my imagination, but this night was the worst of any other night. I had to call hospice.

I had to hold his recliner down from behind. He kept trying to get up, and this way, he couldn't reach me. He also wasn't able to get out of the chair. He would drift off to sleep, but when I let go of the chair, it was as if he knew I had let go. He would try to get out, I would put my whole body onto the top of the recliner to keep him in, and he would keep trying to get out. I told the nurse just to walk in, no more ringing the bell.

When the nurse walked in, she saw me sitting on the head of the recliner and started to laugh. "This is how you are keeping him from getting up?"

I couldn't help laughing too, and I said, "Yes, he doesn't know I'm holding it down so he can't get out of the lying position. It wears him out, but I think I broke the chair."

Just then, the nurse got a text message saying the bed was here. My arms and legs couldn't have been happier. I had been trying to keep him down for hours. The nurse took over for a while and decided to change Tim into his pajamas. He hadn't been in them for a while, and she thought it would make him more comfortable. She told me to go lie down for a little while, that she would get him into bed and comfortable for the night.

I could hear her talking on her phone, and all of a sudden Tim was standing over me, asking what I was doing. It was time to leave for the train station.

I jumped up and reminded him he had to wait for my mom.

He answered, "No, she isn't coming."

As I led him back to his recliner, I heard the nurse ask, "Why did you get him up?"

I explained to her that I didn't—that he had wandered back to me. She couldn't believe with the medicine he was on that he was doing anything but sleeping. I tried to explain it to her, that nothing seemed to be helping.

She said, "I have a cream that I will send over. I guarantee you, he will sleep through the night."

As the bed was getting set up, Tim slept through the noise. It was always curious to me that he would sleep and be content when others were around, but this was the way it had been for a while, and I was getting used to it. The nurse helped me get the sheets on the bed, and we tried to move Tim over, but he wasn't going into that bed. He starting fighting and pushing back.

Then the doorbell rang. I didn't know who it could be at ten o'clock in the evening. The nurse looked at me and said, "It's the cream I was telling you about."

I went to the door, and the man handed me this little package. I thought, *There isn't enough cream in here to get me through the night.* I brought it in to the nurse, and she said, "Wow, they sent over a big bottle." I thought she was trying to be funny, but then she said, "This will last forever. You only need the size of a dime."

I couldn't wait to see what this was going to do.

She convinced Tim to lie down on the bed. She put gloves on and said to me, "Don't touch this cream or the area you rub it on. It's strong, and you'll be asleep within minutes." As she rubbed it on Tim's chest, I could see the calmness coming over him, and I wondered why they hadn't brought this over a few days ago.

We sat talking for a few minutes. She said that she had to leave, but another nurse was going to come over around midnight to sit with Tim while I got some rest. I was surprised they hadn't done that before. I did need the rest.

After the nurse left, for the first time, I felt comfortable being alone with Tim. I thought I could fall asleep. Then the television turned on. I looked over at it, and I looked over at Tim, thinking maybe he had the remote, but it was by the recliner. I understood that a lot of spiritual activity was going on.

I got up to check on Tim. He seemed okay, but the electricity going through my body was telling me something different.

I turned the television off and sat in the quiet, tears rolling down my cheeks. So many things in my life weren't making sense. I'd never thought, after I had met the man of my dreams, that I'd be only fifty years old and about to be a widow. I was sure when we met that he would outlive me, with all of my health problems, but I was now sitting here knowing that what I thought was going to happen wasn't the way it was supposed to be.

I dozed off for a few minutes. The sound of the front door opening woke me up. I knew it was the hospice nurse. I had gotten so used to them walking in and out that it didn't even startle me anymore. She walked into the room, and Tim was still lying comfortably; he hadn't moved in a couple of hours. I went over and kissed his cheek—I was really checking to see if he was still breathing, but I didn't want the nurse to know what I was doing.

The nurse who had come over to give me a break was one I hadn't met before. She was outgoing and seemed to be very caring. We talked for a while, and then she said, "You'd better go get some sleep. I have to leave around four a.m. That only gives you a few hours." I was reluctant, but I knew she was right.

I went to go lie down in the living room. That way, I would be close to the den, but I could still lie in the dark and get some rest. I had been lying down for about twenty minutes and had started to doze off when I got a chill. As I opened my eyes, the room was glowing with a golden light. I focused my eyes and realized that I was seeing angels appear before me, and the beauty and peacefulness that came over me will be with me forever.

I quietly got up and went in to check on Tim. The nurse was sitting in the corner, reading a book. She asked me sharply why I wasn't resting.

I told her that I felt angels, and they were coming to take Tim. His mother and father were also there.

She set her book down and said, "I am a very spiritual person, but your husband probably has weeks before he is going anywhere."

I knew better. I had been around when others had passed and had felt this feeling. I had never seen the angels like I did this time. I knew she was wrong.

I sat down in Tim's recliner and started to cry. The nurse came over and comforted me, telling me I was just overtired and that she only had a little bit of time before she had to leave. She said, "Just lie here in the recliner and close your eyes."

As I closed my eyes, I could feel the angels, and I drifted off to sleep. It seemed as if only a few minutes had passed when she woke me. She said that Tim's oxygen was low, so she'd turned it up, and not to give him any more medicine until five. She had given him everything, and I could probably go back to sleep.

I thanked her, and she left.

I stood to go get a drink of water. Tim was making a very strange noise. It wasn't the "death rattle" I had heard from his father. It was as if he was mumbling, and I figured he was talking in his sleep. I wasn't sure what this cream did, but he was comfortable. Maybe the nurse was right. I fell back asleep, but fifteen minutes later, I was awakened by a crashing noise.

I jumped up. I couldn't find anything, but I noticed that Tim was a little blue. I turned up his oxygen and just sat and watched him breathe. He was barely breathing. I sat on the bed and held his hand.

Sitting there, I could feel the angels and knew it was getting close. I put a call in to hospice and left a message. I went back to holding Tim's hand, and a smile came across his face, a true smile that I hadn't seen since he was diagnosed with Parkinson's. I could tell he was leaving me. He was leaving behind all of his physical ailments. At 4:44 a.m., he was gone. As I sat by myself, I realized that this would be the way that things would be.

Hospice called me back a little after five, and I told them that he had passed. The woman on the other end of the line asked if anyone was with me. I said, "Just my Angels." She told me she would get someone over there as soon as she could.

The social worker and nurse showed up at about six a.m. I told them what time he'd passed, and the nurse said, "We have to use the time when we call his death," which was six a.m. This disappointed me because the day was 4-14-2014 and Tim had passed at 4:44 a.m., all Angel numbers that I had believed in for a long time.

CHAPTER 26

I t was early, and no one had expected that Tim would pass away so quickly, especially me. I hadn't even thought about it until the day before. I know so many people lose their loved ones without any notice, but I needed to make some decisions, and it had to be quick.

Hospice was to call the mortuary to come and pick up Tim. He would be cremated, and I wanted all of the children to see him and be able to have some closure, so I asked if we could leave him in the bed until I could get everyone over to see him. My first call again was to my daughter that lived out of town. She would have a three-hour drive, and I knew it would be a hard three hours as she hadn't seen her dad in a couple of months. I told her I hadn't let her mother know yet, but I would text her when we hung up. I knew that our youngest, whose mother hadn't allowed her to come and visit, would need this closure, even though when she'd seen him last, she'd told him she loved him, and I had been texting her to keep her updated. I was going to let her mom tell her in person that her dad had passed away. I then called the others as I knew they all would be getting ready for work, telling them that I was leaving their father where he was so they could say goodbye, and we could be together as a family for one last time.

Hospice had scheduled a pickup for two p.m. That was the latest they could pick up before the body started to decompose. Everyone got to the house in time, except for the youngest one, whose mother wouldn't allow her to come. This was so hard for me because I knew that one day, our daughter would regret not having that time. As her mother had told me, however, the minute she heard Tim had passed, I was no longer a part of her children's lives. Even though I knew in my heart I would always be a part of their lives, this was probably the most hurtful thing that has ever been said to me, especially only hours after my husband had passed away.

Everyone including aunts and uncles came to the house to pay their last respects. The sadness of losing such a great man who had touched so many lives was overwhelming.

I was shaking on the inside. I was in denial, but I was also angry and still trying to hide these feelings as I looked at the four children that sat around their father with tears in their eyes. I knew I would never know how they felt, but I had to be strong and be there for them as long as they needed me.

The funeral was twenty days later as his brother and sister-in-law had only left four days earlier, and the second to the youngest had finals for school. I tried to do what would be convenient for everyone. It wasn't easy, but it worked out the way it was supposed to and gave everyone a chance to be there.

As we sat in the church, I looked behind me and realized that over two hundred people had come for the service—relatives, friends, and even old customers jammed into the pews and celebrated Tim's life. The kids from the FFA made flowers for the service and the reception after, and everything was perfect.

Tim was loved, and everyone showed up not only physically but spiritually. The day was blessed with memories of love and even forgiveness. This was the first time I would see the mother of the two youngest that Tim had brought into my life thirteen years earlier.

AFTERWORD

This life experience changed my life forever, and I knew that one day I would write about it as I had kept a journal. A few months ago, I was going to burn those memories to try and help me get past the loss, but I realized that this could help so many others.

Helping your loved one isn't easy, especially when you know something is wrong, while unsure what it is. This is a familiar feeling to those who watch loved ones suffer from chronic illnesses. Doctor visits for tests and exams become frequent, and finally the doctor's appointment you have been waiting for arrives, as does the nervousness and the need for answers. Sometimes, receiving the first set of answers results in yet another set of questions, and if you are a family caregiver, you most likely understand this all too well. Sometimes, the questions never stop.

When a loved one is first diagnosed with any disease, you will probably have a lot of questions. Becoming informed requires searching for information from trustworthy organizations and is always the best method of preparation to help make decisions with confidence. With any health issue, asking questions is a must.

You don't know, if you don't ask.

Some resources, like the National Institute of Health, can be a great place to start for any chronic illness. They have links on their web pages that can help lead you in the right direction. For example, for Parkinson's, the Parkinson's Disease Foundation, the National

Parkinson Foundation, and the American Parkinson Disease Association can help you become more familiar with this disease. Become an advocate and ask questions for the benefit of your loved one, yourself, and your family. But make sure the person who has been diagnosed is aware that you are doing this with them and that you are there to support and help guide them.

Some of these tips are for things to know when you are going to visit a doctor or specialist. Take this list with you, and write down the answers:

- Bring someone else with you. If you are the patient, it helps to have another person hear what is said and think of questions to ask, especially if you are the one being diagnosed. You will need the support.

- Write out your questions ahead of time so you don't forget them.

- Write down the answers you get, and make sure you understand what you are hearing. Ask for clarification, if necessary.

- Don't be afraid to ask your questions or ask where you can find more information about what you are discussing. You have a right to know.

- Are my symptoms compatible with a diagnosis of Parkinson's disease? (Or whatever the diagnosis has been.)

- Is there any chance that my symptoms are caused by something reversible?

- Are my children at risk for Parkinson's disease? (Or whatever the diagnosis has been.) This is critical for other family members. They will want to know if it is genetic.

- Are there lifestyle changes I can make?

- Will I need medications?

- What are the statistics on improvement with various medications?

- Could my medications interact with any other medications I'm taking?

- Are there any clinical trials that I could participate in?

- Are there surgical procedures that might help me? What are the statistics after surgery?

- Am I a candidate for any of those surgical procedures?

- When should I consider surgical procedures?

- Are there any alternative or complementary therapies that would help my symptoms?

- Should I change my diet?

- What kinds of exercises might benefit me?

- Might I benefit from physical therapy?

- Can I continue to drive?

- Can you direct me to a professional who can help me learn stress-reduction techniques?

- Are there any support groups for people with Parkinson's disease in my community?

- What is the usual progression of symptoms in Parkinson's disease? (Or whatever the diagnosis has been.)

- Will I need to go to a nursing home? This is a hard one, but getting the answer can make your decisions easier to make.

- Is there any way to predict how severe my symptoms may become?

- Is there any way to predict how much disability I might experience?

- Are there any support groups for me?

- Are there any support groups for my family and loved ones?

Once you have the answers to these questions, you will have enough information to help with putting together a care plan that can benefit the whole family. When you have questions that don't get answered, they stay in your mind, and you will continue to be confused until they get answered. Never be afraid to ask!

Caregiving Tips

For most of us that have had to become a caregiver, it wasn't by choice. We have had a friend or loved one that has become ill and needs this type of care. This role can be very difficult, not only emotionally but physically. These tips will help you to be able to adjust to this new task. Remember that everyone needs help, including the caregiver.

- Offering the love and support necessary to meet the challenges of a chronic illness isn't only physical but also emotional. Try to get help if you need it.

- Help to maintain the quality of life for both you and your loved one. This is vital for your relationship. It keeps the patient feeling that life is still good even though it has changed.

- Educate yourself about symptoms, treatments, and the progression of the disease. That way, you'll understand what changes to expect in your loved one's behavior or symptoms and how you can best help when those changes occur.

- Keep track of all the appointments with the doctor. For medication schedules, using a pill organizer can help. Especially don't forget about exercise.

- Set realistic goals. Don't attempt to do everything. By setting attainable goals, you are setting everyone up for success rather than disappointment.

- Don't put your life on hold. Continue to meet with friends, participate in hobbies or groups, and maintain as normal a schedule as possible. Not only will you feel more energized, but you will be less likely to feel resentful.

- Have someone you can talk to. You are there to listen to and support your loved one, but you also need a support person. Talk openly and honestly with a friend or family member. If that's not possible, join a support group, one for the illness and one for the caregiver. Understanding that you aren't alone and that someone else is in a similar situation helps you to feel nurtured.

- Take time for yourself. Make sure you have time to relax. If necessary, enlist the help of other family members or even hire someone to assist you in providing care. This is a must: if you don't take care of yourself and you get sick, who will take care of your loved one?

AUTHOR BIOGRAPHY

Holly Bird was born and raised in Tempe, Arizona. She is a best-selling, award winning, contributor and author. Her life experiences include motivational speaking, spiritual mentoring, marriage, gardening, cooking, and traveling. She shares this and more, on her blog and social media. She has worked in marketing and sales, where education and speaking are her specialty. You can work with or even follow Holly's journey at:

Blog
www.Hollysbirdnest.com

Email
HollyBird@hollysbirdnest.com

Facebook
https://www.facebook.com/hollysbirdnest/
https://www.facebook.com/loveyourangels/

Twitter
https://twitter.com/hollyjbird

ACKNOWLEDGMENTS

To Shanda Trofe of Transcendent Publishing, I thank you for your guidance and belief in me. With the help of my editor, Jean Hall, you both have made this book possible so that others may learn from the experiences that I had to share.

To my many relatives, both mine and the Bird family and all of my friends who have stood by me in times that I have struggled, and who help support me with love and compassion, I thank you with all my heart, you are a true blessing in my life.

49747295R00087

Made in the USA
Columbia, SC
26 January 2019